致敬译界巨匠许渊冲先生

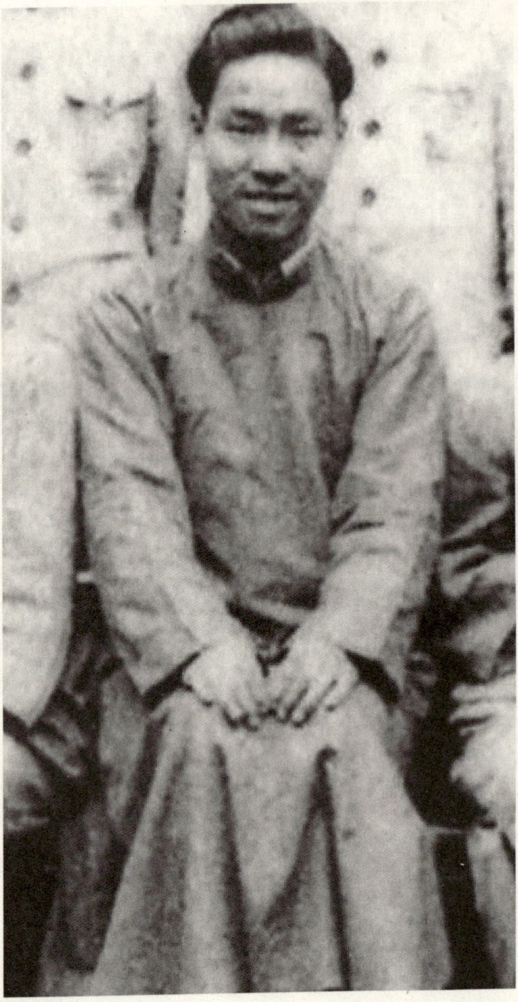

许渊冲译
元曲三百首
300 YUAN SONGS

译

许渊冲

中国出版集团
中译出版社

目录
Contents

I		译序	
002	元好问 Yuan Haowen	人月圆 Tune: Man and Moon	
006	元好问 Yuan Haowen	小圣乐 Tune: Minor Sacred Music	
010	杨 果 Yang Guo	小桃红 Tune: Red Peach Blossoms	
014	刘秉忠 Liu Bingzhong	干荷叶 Tune: Dried Lotus Leaves	
020	杜仁杰 Du Renjie	耍孩儿 Tune: Teasing the Child	
036	王和卿 Wang Heqing	醉中天 Tune: A Drinker's Sky	
038	王和卿 Wang Heqing	一半儿 Tune: Half and Half	
042	盍西村 He Xicun	小桃红 Tune: Red Peach Blossoms	
044	盍西村 He Xicun	小桃红 Tune: Red Peach Blossoms	
046	盍西村 He Xicun	小桃红 Tune: Red Peach Blossoms	
048	商 挺 Shang Ting	潘妃曲 Tune: Song of Princess Pan	
050	胡祗遹 Hu Zhiyu	沉醉东风 Tune: Intoxicated in East Wind	
052	伯 颜 Bo Yan	喜春来 Tune: Welcome to Spring	

054	王 恽 Wang Yun	平湖乐 Tune: Joy of Calm Lake
056	卢 挚 Lu Zhi	节节高 Tune: Higher and Higher
058	卢 挚 Lu Zhi	沉醉东风 Tune: Intoxicated in East Wind
060	卢 挚 Lu Zhi	沉醉东风 Tune: Intoxicated in East Wind
062	卢 挚 Lu Zhi	沉醉东风 Tune: Intoxicated in East Wind
064	卢 挚 Lu Zhi	蟾宫曲 Tune: Song of Moon Palace
066	卢 挚 Lu Zhi	蟾宫曲 Tune: Song of Moon Palace
068	卢 挚 Lu Zhi	殿前欢 Tune: Joy before Palace
070	陈草庵 Chen Cao'an	山坡羊 Tune: Sheep on the Slope
072	关汉卿 Guan Hanqing	白鹤令 Tune: Song of White Crane
074	关汉卿 Guan Hanqing	四块玉 Tune: Four Pieces of Jade
076	关汉卿 Guan Hanqing	四块玉 Tune: Four Pieces of Jade
080	关汉卿 Guan Hanqing	沉醉东风 Tune: Intoxicated in East Wind
082	关汉卿 Guan Hanqing	大德歌 Tune: Song of Great Virtue

086	关汉卿 Guan Hanqing	碧玉箫 Tune: Green Jade Flute
090	关汉卿 Guan Hanqing	一枝花 Tune: A Sprig of Flowers
104	白 朴 Bai Pu	寄生草 Tune: Parasite Grass
106	白 朴 Bai Pu	阳春曲 Tune: Song of Spring
108	白 朴 Bai Pu	天净沙 Tune: Sunny Sand
112	白 朴 Bai Pu	沉醉东风 Tune: Intoxicated in East Wind
114	姚 燧 Yao Sui	醉高歌 Tune: Drinking Song
116	姚 燧 Yao Sui	凭阑人寄征衣 Tune: Leaning on Balustrade
118	庾天赐 Yu Tianci	雁儿落过得胜令 From "Falling Swan" to "Triumphant Song"
120	刘敏中 Liu Minzhong	黑漆弩 Tune: Varnished Black Bow
122	马致远 Ma Zhiyuan	四块玉 Tune: Four Pieces of Jade
124	马致远 Ma Zhiyuan	四块玉 Tune: Four Pieces of Jade
126	马致远 Ma Zhiyuan	天净沙 Tune: Sunny Sand
128	马致远 Ma Zhiyuan	清江引 Tune: Song of Clear River

130	马致远 Ma Zhiyuan	寿阳曲 Tune: Song of Long-lived Sun
134	马致远 Ma Zhiyuan	夜行船 Night-sailing Boat
144	马致远 Ma Zhiyuan	寿阳曲 Tune: Song of Long-lived Sun
146	赵孟頫 Zhao Mengfu	后庭花 Tune: Backyard Flowers
148	王实甫 Wang Shifu	十二月过尧民歌 From "A Year's End" to "Folklore"
150	滕宾 Teng Bin	普天乐 Tune: Universal Joy
152	邓玉宾 Deng Yubin	叨叨令 Tune: Chattering Song
154	邓玉宾 Deng Yubin	叨叨令 Tune: Chattering Song
156	阿利西瑛 Ali Xiying	殿前欢 Tune: Joy before Palace
158	冯子振 Feng Zizhen	鹦鹉曲 Tune: Song of Parrot
160	冯子振 Feng Zizhen	鹦鹉曲 Tune: Song of Parrot
162	朱帘秀 Zhu Lianxiu	寿阳曲 Tune: Song of Long-lived Sun
164	贯云石 Guan Yunshi	塞鸿秋 Tune: Autumn Swan on Frontier
166	贯云石 Guan Yunshi	红绣鞋 Tune: Embroidered Red Shoes

168	贯云石 Guan Yunshi	落梅风 Tune: Wind of Falling Mume Blossoms
170	贯云石 Guan Yunshi	蟾宫曲 Tune: Song of Moon Palace
172	贯云石 Guan Yunshi	清江引 Tune: Song of Clear River
174	张养浩 Zhang Yanghao	得胜令 Tune: Triumphant Song
176	张养浩 Zhang Yanghao	水仙子 Tune: Song of Daffodils
178	张养浩 Zhang Yanghao	山坡羊 Tune: Sheep on the Slope
180	张养浩 Zhang Yanghao	朝天子 Tune: Skyward Song
182	白贲 Bai Ben	鹦鹉曲 Tune: Song of Parrot
184	郑光祖 Zheng Guangzu	蟾宫曲 Tune: Song of Moon Palace
188	曾瑞 Zeng Rui	闺中闻杜鹃 Hearing the Cuckoo in My Boudoir
194	曾瑞 Zeng Rui	集贤宾 Tune: Meeting of Good Friends
204	睢景臣 Ju Jingchen	哨遍 Tune: Whistling Around
220	周文质 Zhou Wenzhi	叨叨令 Tune: Chattering Song
222	周文质 Zhou Wenzhi	塞儿令 Tune: Song of Frontier

224	乔 吉 Qiao Ji	清江引 Tune: Song of Clear River
226	乔 吉 Qiao Ji	清江引 Tune: Song of Clear River
228	乔 吉 Qiao Ji	山坡羊 Tune: Sheep on the Slope
234	乔 吉 Qiao Ji	卖花声 Tune: Song of a Flower Seller
236	乔 吉 Qiao Ji	凭阑人 Tune: Leaning on Balustrade
240	乔 吉 Qiao Ji	折桂令 Tune: Plucking Laurel Branch
248	乔 吉 Qiao Ji	满庭芳 Tune: Courtyard Full of Fragrance
252	乔 吉 Qiao Ji	殿前欢 Tune: Joy before Palace
254	乔 吉 Qiao Ji	小桃红 Tune: Red Peach Blossoms
256	乔 吉 Qiao Ji	水仙子 Tune: Song of Daffodils
258	乔 吉 Qiao Ji	水仙子 Tune: Song of Daffodils
260	乔 吉 Qiao Ji	雁儿落过得胜令 From "Falling Swan" to "Triumphant Song"
264	乔 吉 Qiao Ji	集贤宾 Tune: Meeting of Good Friends
272	刘时中 Liu Shizhong	殿前欢 Tune: Joy before Palace

274	阿鲁威 A Luwei	落梅风 Tune: Wind of Falling Mume Blossoms
276	王元鼎 Wang Yuanding	醉太平 Tune: Drunk in Time of Peace
278	薛昂夫 Xue Angfu	塞鸿秋 Tune: Autumn Swan on Frontier
280	薛昂夫 Xue Angfu	楚天遥过清江引 From "Far-flung Southern Sky" to "Song of Clear River"
284	吴弘道 Wu Hongdao	金字经 Tune: Golden Canon
288	吴弘道 Wu Hongdao	拨不断 Tune: Unbroken String
290	赵善庆 Zhao Shanqing	沉醉东风 Tune: Intoxicated in East Wind
292	赵善庆 Zhao Shanqing	折桂令 Tune: Plucking Laurel Branch
294	赵善庆 Zhao Shanqing	庆东原 Tune: Blessed East Plain
296	马谦斋 Ma Qianzhai	柳营曲 Tune: Song of Willow Camp
298	张可久 Zhang Kejiu	人月圆 Tune: Man and Moon
300	张可久 Zhang Kejiu	人月圆 Tune: Man and Moon
302	张可久 Zhang Kejiu	人月圆 Tune: Man and Moon

304	张可久 Zhang Kejiu	醉太平 Tune: Drunk in Time of Peace
306	张可久 Zhang Kejiu	醉太平 Tune: Drunk in Time of Peace
308	张可久 Zhang Kejiu	锦橙梅 Tune: Orange and Mume on Brocade
310	张可久 Zhang Kejiu	迎仙客 Tune: Greeting a Fairy Guest
312	张可久 Zhang Kejiu	红绣鞋 Tune: Embroidered Red Shoes
314	张可久 Zhang Kejiu	红绣鞋 Tune: Embroidered Red Shoes
316	张可久 Zhang Kejiu	梧叶儿 Tune: Plane Leaves
318	张可久 Zhang Kejiu	梧叶儿 Tune: Plane Leaves
320	张可久 Zhang Kejiu	折桂令 Tune: Plucking Laurel Branch
322	张可久 Zhang Kejiu	折桂令 Tune: Plucking Laurel Branch
324	张可久 Zhang Kejiu	折桂令 Tune: Plucking Laurel Branch
326	张可久 Zhang Kejiu	折桂令 Tune: Plucking Laurel Branch
328	张可久 Zhang Kejiu	水仙子 Tune: Song of Daffodils
330	张可久 Zhang Kejiu	小桃红 Tune: Red Peach Blossoms

332	张可久 Zhang Kejiu	普天乐 Tune: Universal Joy	
334	张可久 Zhang Kejiu	普天乐 Tune: Universal Joy	
336	张可久 Zhang Kejiu	喜春来 Tune: Welcome to Spring	
338	张可久 Zhang Kejiu	喜春来 Tune: Welcome to Spring	
340	张可久 Zhang Kejiu	朝天子 Tune: Skyward Song	
342	张可久 Zhang Kejiu	山坡羊 Tune: Sheep on the Slope	
344	张可久 Zhang Kejiu	殿前欢 Tune: Joy before Palace	
346	张可久 Zhang Kejiu	清江引 Tune: Song of Clear River	
348	张可久 Zhang Kejiu	天净沙 Tune: Sunny Sand	
350	张可久 Zhang Kejiu	一枝花 Tune: A Sprig of Flowers	
358	张可久 Zhang Kejiu	凭阑人 Tune: Leaning on Balustrade	
360	徐再思 Xu Zaisi	普天乐 Tune: Universal Joy	
362	徐再思 Xu Zaisi	喜春来 Tune: Welcome to Spring	
364	徐再思 Xu Zaisi	蟾宫曲 Tune: Song of Moon Palace	

366	徐再思 Xu Zaisi	蟾宫曲	Tune: Song of Moon Palace
368	徐再思 Xu Zaisi	水仙子	Tune: Song of Daffodils
370	徐再思 Xu Zaisi	水仙子	Tune: Song of Daffodils
372	徐再思 Xu Zaisi	人月圆	Tune: Man and Moon
374	徐再思 Xu Zaisi	朝天子	Tune: Skyward Song
376	查德卿 Zha Deqing	一半儿	Tune: Half and Half
378	查德卿 Zha Deqing	柳营曲	Tune: Song of Willow Camp
380	唐毅夫 Tang Yifu	一枝花	Tune: A Sprig of Flowers
388	朱庭玉 Zhu Tingyu	天净沙	Tune: Sunny Sand
390	张鸣善 Zhang Mingshan	普天乐	Tune: Universal Joy
392	张鸣善 Zhang Mingshan	普天乐	Tune: Universal Joy
394	张鸣善 Zhang Mingshan	普天乐	Tune: Universal Joy
396	杨朝英 Yang Chaoying	水仙子	Tune: Song of Daffodils
398	宋方壶 Song Fanghu	山坡羊	Tune: Sheep on the Slope

400	宋方壶 Song Fanghu	清江引 Tune: Song of Clear River
402	宋方壶 Song Fanghu	斗鹌鹑 Tune: Fight of Quails
414	贾固 Jia Gu	醉高歌过红绣鞋 From "Drinking Song" to "Embroidered Red Shoes"
418	周德清 Zhou Deqing	塞鸿秋 Tune: Autumn Swan on Frontier
420	周德清 Zhou Deqing	满庭芳 Tune: Courtyard Full of Fragrance
422	周德清 Zhou Deqing	折桂令 Tune: Plucking Laurel Branch
424	班惟志 Ban Weizhi	一枝花 Tune: A Sprig of Flowers
430	汪元亨 Wang Yuanheng	醉太平 Tune: Drunk in Time of Peace
432	汪元亨 Wang Yuanheng	朝天子 Tune: Skyward Song
434	汪元亨 Wang Yuanheng	沉醉东风 Tune: Intoxicated in East Wind
436	倪瓒 Ni Zan	人月圆 Tune: Man and Moon
438	倪瓒 Ni Zan	小桃红 Tune: Red Peach Blossoms
440	倪瓒 Ni Zan	凭阑人 Tune: Leaning on Balustrade
442	倪瓒 Ni Zan	水仙子 Tune: Song of Daffodils

444	刘庭信 Liu Tingxin	折桂令 Tune: Plucking Laurel Branch
446	刘庭信 Liu Tingxin	水仙子 Tune: Song of Daffodils
450	刘庭信 Liu Tingxin	一枝花 Tune: A Sprig of Flowers
452	汤式 Tang Shi	小梁州 Tune: Minor Frontier
456	汤式 Tang Shi	天香引 Tune: Song of Celestial Fragrance
458	兰楚芳 Lan Chufang	四块玉 Tune: Four Pieces of Jade
462	钟嗣成 Zhong Sicheng	醉太平 Tune: Intoxicated in Time of Peace
466	钱霖 Qian Lin	哨遍 Tune: Whistling Around
490	孙周卿 Sun Zhouqing	蟾宫曲 Tune: Song of Moon Palace
492	曹德 Cao De	庆东原 Tune: Blessed Eastern Plain
494	真氏 Zhen Shi	解三酲 Tune: Thrice Drunk and Sobered
496	吴西逸 Wu Xiyi	天净沙 Tune: Sunny Sand
498	吴西逸 Wu Xiyi	清江引 Tune: Song of the Clear River
500	吴西逸 Wu Xiyi	寿阳曲 Tune: Song of Long-lived Sun

502	程景初 Cheng Jingchu	醉太平 Tune: Drunk in Time of Peace
504	无名氏 Anonymous	水仙子 Tune: Song of Daffodils
510	无名氏 Anonymous	折桂令 Tune: Plucking Laurel Branch
512	无名氏 Anonymous	折桂令 Tune: Plucking Laurel Branch
514	无名氏 Anonymous	塞鸿秋 Tune: Autumn Swan on Frontier
516	无名氏 Anonymous	塞鸿秋 Tune: Autumn Swan on Frontier
518	无名氏 Anonymous	梧叶儿 Tune: Plane Leaves
520	无名氏 Anonymous	梧叶儿 Tune: Plane Leaves
522	无名氏 Anonymous	四换头 Tune: Changes of Tunes
524	无名氏 Anonymous	四换头 Tune: Changes of Tunes
526	无名氏 Anonymous	红绣鞋 Tune: Embroidered Red Shoes
528	无名氏 Anonymous	红绣鞋 Tune: Embroidered Red Shoes
530	无名氏 Anonymous	红绣鞋 Tune: Embroidered Red Shoes
532	无名氏 Anonymous	红绣鞋 Tune: Embroidered Red Shoes

534	无名氏 Anonymous	庆宣和 Tune: Celebration of Imperial Reign
536	无名氏 Anonymous	沉醉东风 Tune: Intoxicated in East Wind
540	无名氏 Anonymous	塞儿令 Tune: Song of Frontier
542	无名氏 Anonymous	上小楼 Tune: Ascending the Attic
544	无名氏 Anonymous	寄生草 Tune: Parasite Grass
546	无名氏 Anonymous	快活三过朝天子四换头 From "Happy Three" to "Changes of Tunes"
552	无名氏 Anonymous	阅金经 Tune: Reading Golden Classics
554	无名氏 Anonymous	普天乐 Tune: Universal Joy
556	无名氏 Anonymous	雁儿落过得胜令 From "Falling Swan" to "Triumphant Song"
558	无名氏 Anonymous	叨叨令 Tune: Chattering Song
560	无名氏 Anonymous	叨叨令 Tune: Chattering Song
562	无名氏 Anonymous	游四门 Tune: The Four Gates Visited
566	无名氏 Anonymous	三番玉楼人 Tune: Thrice in Jade Pavilion
568	无名氏 Anonymous	朝天子 Tune: Skyward Song

570	无名氏 Anonymous	叨叨令 Tune: Chattering Song
572	无名氏 Anonymous	红绣鞋 Tune: Embroidered Red Shoes
574	无名氏 Anonymous	喜春来 Tune: Welcome to Spring
576	无名氏 Anonymous	快活三过朝天子四换头 From "Happy Three" to "Changes of Tunes"
582	无名氏 Anonymous	骂玉郎过感皇恩采茶歌 From "Blaming My Gallant" to "Tea-picking Song"

译　序

"一个国家人民文化水平的高低，要看它对人类文化的贡献，也就是说，它对世界文化提供了多少珍品。"（引自1982年11月17日《人民日报》）唐诗、宋词、元曲就是我国对人类文化提供的珍品。

诗言志。孔子说过："诗可以兴，可以观，可以群，可以怨。"这就是说，"言志"包括见物起兴，观察反映，合群交流，发泄怨愤。而在唐诗、宋词、元曲中，我们可以看到"兴观群怨"的丰富内容。如以唐诗而论，李白的浪漫主义诗篇中有人与自然的交流，杜甫的现实主义诗篇中有对战乱时代的反映，白居易通俗易懂的诗篇中有对世风的批评，李商隐的象征主义诗篇中有心灵的呼声。如以宋词而论，则有抒情缠绵悱恻的柳永、以理化情的苏轼、语浅情深的李清照、愤世嫉俗的辛弃疾。一方面，唐诗和宋词都继承了《诗经》中"兴观群怨"的文学传统；另一方面，又对元代散曲产生了重大的影响。

唐宋两朝是中国历史上的黄金时代，600年间经济繁荣，文化发达，在全世界是首屈一指的。而当时的西方正处在黑暗时期。到了元代，蒙古族从北南下，侵入中原，统治全国，君临天下，压迫南方人民。现实生活中，蒙古人甚至可以随意杀死南人而不受惩罚，知识分子却沦落到了非常低贱的地位，甚至在妓女之下，只在乞丐之上。这种现象在元散曲中都有反映。如钟嗣成在《醉太平》中描写乞丐：

> 绕前街后街，
> 进大院深宅，
> 怕有那慈悲好善小裙钗，
> 请乞儿一顿饱斋。

又描写穷书生：

> 风流贫最好，
> 村沙富难交。
> 拾灰泥补砌了旧砖窑，
> 开一个教乞儿市学。
> 裹一顶半新不旧乌纱帽，
> 穿一领半长不短黄麻罩。
> 系一条半联不断皂环绦，
> 做一个穷风月训导。

又如真氏写一个妓女说：

> 对人前乔做作娇模样，
> 背地里泪千行。

由此可以看出唐代诗人的现实主义,到了元代,已经深入下层人民了。

元代知识分子一般无力积极反抗,只会愤愤不平地发发牢骚,以怨天尤人的方式发泄心中不平。如无名氏的《朝天子》中说:

> 不读书有权,
> 不识字有钱、
> 不晓事倒有人夸荐。
> 老天只任忩心偏,
> 贤和愚无分辨。

发牢骚后,他们尽量麻醉自己,把乐天知命,知足不辱当作处世的原则;把人生无常,消极的出世思想渗入自己的作品,主观幻想地美化田园的隐居生活。如冯子振在《鹦鹉曲》中写道:

> 嵯峨峰顶移家住,
> ……
> 指门前万叠云山,
> 是不费青蚨买处。

他们做伴的是渔樵,流连的是诗酒,享受的是自然风光、田园乐趣,追求的生活境界是任情适意、逍遥自在。如乔吉在《满庭芳》中说:

> 白云流水无人禁,

> 胜似山林。
> 钓晚霞寒波濯锦,
> 看秋潮夜海溶金。

但是在自然风光中,他们并不能逃避现实,还是会遇到惊涛骇浪、废墟荒冢,使他们回到现实中来。如张养浩在《山坡羊》中写道:

> 峰峦如聚,
> 波涛如怒,
> ……
> 宫阙万间都做了土。
> 兴,
> 百姓苦;
> 亡,
> 百姓苦。

在自然中得不到安慰,有的诗人只好发思古之幽情,借古人的酒杯,浇胸中的块垒。如周德清在《满庭芳·看岳王传》中说:

> 功成却被权臣妒,
> 正落奸谋。
> ……
> 钱塘路,
> 愁风怨雨,
> 长是洒西湖。

在元曲中,我们可以看到唐代的英雄主义已经蜕化为悲观思想。宋代的理性主义已经转变成消极无为,他们抒发的情感大众化了,但他们的批评精神依然存在,他们的语体文风却有新的发展。

以内容而论,元曲主要的题材是叹世和归隐;以形式而论,唱词多半用的是老百姓的日常口语。宋代的李清照早已用口语入词,如著名的《如梦令》:

> 知否,知否?
> 应是绿肥红瘦。

但李清照的口语还比较高雅,我们再读张可久的《山坡羊·闺思》,那的确是用语浅而意思极真了:

> 掩春闺一觉伤春睡,
> 柳花飞,
> 小琼姬,
> 一声"雪下呈祥瑞",
> 团圆梦儿生唤起。
> "谁,
> 不做美?
> 呸,
> 却是你!"

元曲和唐诗、宋词不同的地方,是诗词韵分平仄,不能错押,有时可以转韵。曲则没有入声,平上去三声通押,一韵到底。而且用韵的密度较大，有时甚至是每句一韵。诗词尽量避免字句的重复，尤其是不能重韵，而曲却往往以重韵见长。元曲和诗词最大的不同，是曲在正规的格调之外，还可以加上一些衬字，使作者有更大的自由。这说明元曲比诗词更加解放、更加先进，可以说是诗词的发展。只要比较同一首曲子却有两种字数不等的曲调，就可以看出。如徐再思的《水仙子》：

> 九分恩爱九分忧，
> 两处相思两处愁，
> 十年迤逗十年受。
> 几遍成几遍休，
> 半点事半点惭羞，
> 三秋恨三秋感旧，
> 三春怨三春病酒，
> 一世害一世风流。

这首曲子只有8行55个字，而刘庭信的《水仙子》却有29行100个字，由此可见刘曲比徐曲多了21行，45个字，如前四行：

> 恨重叠，
> 重叠恨，
> 恨绵绵，
> 恨满晚妆楼。

这几行就是把"重叠恨满晚妆楼"1行7个字扩大成为4行

14个字，增加的字和原来一行的字数相等，由此可见元曲衬字特点之一斑。

唐宋的律诗都以对仗见长，如杜甫"古今七律第一"的《登高》中最著名的一联：

> 无边落木萧萧下，
> 不尽长江滚滚来。

到了元代，对仗的种类也增加了，如"鼎足对"，就是诗词中所没有的。它以三句为一组，互为对仗，往往形成对事物淋漓尽致的刻画，这又是诗词的发展。如马致远《夜行船》煞尾中的三句：

> 看密匝匝蚁排兵，
> 乱纷纷蜂酿蜜，
> 急攘攘蝇争血。

元曲可分散曲和杂剧两大类，散曲又可分小令、带过曲、套曲三类。小令只有一支曲子，带过曲是由两三支小令组成的，如《雁儿落过得胜令》由《雁儿落》和《得胜令》两支小令组成，《骂玉郎过感皇恩采茶歌》由《骂玉郎》《感皇恩》和《采茶歌》三支小令组成，所以可算是短套曲。套曲一般由四支小令以上组成，如杜仁杰的《耍孩儿》套曲由七支曲子组成，主题是《庄家不识构阑》，写乡下人进城看戏，颇像白居易现实主义的乐府。关汉卿的《一枝花》套曲却只包括四支曲子，主题《不伏老》颇像嬉笑怒骂的辛词。马致远的《夜行船》包括七支曲子，主题《秋思》有苏东坡《赤壁怀古》的意味。曾瑞的《集贤宾》由六支曲子组成，主题颇有缠绵悱恻的柳词风味。睢景臣的《哨遍》包括八支曲子，主题是《高祖还乡》，在君道森严的封建时代，作者能够不从歌功颂德的角度来写汉高祖刘邦"威加海内兮归故乡"的盛况，而从一个过去与他有瓜葛的乡下人眼中，写出他装腔作势的可笑模样，显得非常新奇。乔吉的《集贤宾·咏柳忆别》、张可久的《一枝花·湖上归》、宋方壶的《斗鹌鹑》套曲却都显示了元曲的抒情主流。钱霖的《哨遍》最长，包括12支曲子，主题《看钱奴》却是讽刺为富不仁的守财奴的。从本书选译的300首小令和套曲，可以看出元曲和唐诗、宋词之间的继承和发展的关系。元曲发展的最高阶段是杂剧，最著名的代表作是王实甫的《西厢记》，国外评价很高，说是可和莎士比亚比美，却比莎士比亚早了两三百年，由此可见中国文化之发达。而元曲则和唐诗、宋词一样，都是世界文化的珍品。

总而言之，元曲继承和发展了唐诗和宋词已有的"兴观群怨"的优秀传统：在意美方面，使诗歌更大众化；在音美方面，使韵律更自由化；在形美方面，使格式更多样化了。因此，元曲把诗歌进一步推向通俗化、口语化、灵活化，为近现代的白话文学开辟了道路，可以说是中国新文化运动的一个重要源头。

许渊冲译元曲三百首

人月圆[1]

卜居[2]外家[3]东园

元好问

（一）

重冈[4]已隔红尘[5]断，

村落更年丰。

移居要就：

窗中远岫[6]，

舍后长松。

十年种木，

一年种谷，

都付儿童。

老夫惟有：

醒来明月，

醉后清风。

① 人月圆：曲牌名。
② 卜居：择地而居。
③ 外家：母亲的娘家亲戚。
④ 重冈：重重叠叠的山峦。
⑤ 红尘：本是佛家对人生的称谓，这里指纷扰不止的外部世界。
⑥ 窗中远岫：从窗户中可以看到远处的山峦。

Tune: Man and Moon

Moving to My Mother's East Garden

Yuan Haowen

(I)

Hill on hill keeps apart the vanity fair
From this village of bumper year.
I move house to come near
The window-enframed distant hill
And the pine-trees behind the windowsill.

I'll leave the woods and fields to the care
Of my children dear
So that I may do what I will.
Awake, I'll enjoy the moon so bright;
Drunk, the refreshing breeze so light.

（二）

玄都观里桃千树，
花落水空流①。
凭君莫问：
清泾浊渭②，
去马来牛。

谢公③扶病，
羊昙④挥泪，
一醉都休。
古今几度：
生存华屋，
零落山丘⑤！

① 玄都观里桃千树，花落水空流：唐代刘禹锡《元和十一年自朗州召至京，戏赠看花诸君子》有："玄都观里桃千树，尽是刘郎去后栽。"刘禹锡的诗歌把长安玄都观中由盛而衰的桃花和种桃道士作比，讽刺当时打击革新运动的朝廷新贵和当权者。本曲在此处用这个典故来感叹金朝的盛衰兴亡。
② 清泾浊渭：泾水清，渭水浊。这里指是非分明。
③ 谢公：谢安，东晋著名将领，曾指挥淝水之战大败前秦，最后病死。
④ 羊昙：谢安的外甥，当时名士。谢安死时，他伤心恸哭。
⑤ 古今几度：生存华屋，零落山丘：曹植有"生存华屋处，零落归山丘"之句，意谓纵然生前尽享富贵，死后一样是葬身荒丘。

(II)

In Royal Temple there are thousands of peach trees,
Whence fallen blooms in vain with water flow.
Do not ask, please,
If water is not clear,
Or cows will come or horses go.

What matters if the minister was ill,
And his friend shed tear on tear!
What can I do but drink my fill?
How many splendid houses of olden days appear
Fallen to ruins in the hill!

小圣乐

骤雨打新荷

元好问

（一）

绿叶阴浓，

遍池亭水阁，

偏趁凉多①。

海榴②初绽，

朵朵蹙③红罗。

乳燕雏莺弄语，

有高柳鸣蝉相和。

骤雨过，

珍珠乱撒，

打遍新荷。

---

① 绿叶阴浓，遍池亭水阁，偏趁凉多：指池亭水阁之处特别凉快。趁：追逐。
② 海榴：石榴，花为深红色。
③ 蹙：褶皱的样子。

Tune: Minor Sacred Music

Sudden Shower Beating on New Lotus Leaves

Yuan Haowen

(I)

Green leaves casting deep shade

Over pavilions and bowers by the pool

Bring a delightful cool.

The pomegranates in early flower

Look like frowning red brocade.

Young swallows chirp and orioles warble their song

While cicadas on high willow trees trill along.

A sudden shower

With raindrops like pearls or dew

Beats on lotus leaves new.

（二）

人生百年有几，
念良辰美景，
休放虚过。
穷通前定，
何用苦张罗。
命友邀宾玩赏，
对芳樽浅酌低歌。
且酩酊^①，
任他两轮日月，
来往如梭。

---

① 酩酊：喝得大醉的样子。

(II)

How many people can live to a hundred years?

Do not let golden hours and fine scenery

Slip away!

Our poor destiny

Cannot be turned another way.

It's better to invite friends and enjoy with peers

Good wine and songs we sing low.

Be tipsy while we may,

And let the sun and moon come and go

Like shuttles to and fro!

小桃红①

采莲女

杨 果

（一）

满城烟水月微茫②，

人倚兰舟③唱。

常记相逢若耶④上，

隔三湘⑤，

碧云望断空惆怅。

美人笑道，

莲花相似，

情短藕丝⑥长。

---

① 小桃红：越调曲调，又名"武陵春""采莲曲""绛桃春"。
② "满城"句：水乡月夜的景色一片朦胧。微茫：隐约，模糊。
③ 兰舟：对采莲舟的美称，不一定是用质地坚硬而芳香的木兰制作的船。
④ 若耶：若耶溪，又名浣纱溪，相传是西施浣纱之地。
⑤ 三湘：指湘水与另外三支河流汇合而成的三段江流，一是上游与漓江汇合成的漓湘，二是中游与潇水汇合成的潇湘，三是下游与蒸水汇合成的蒸湘。
⑥ 丝：与"思"构成谐音双关。

Tune: Red Peach Blossoms

The Lotus Gatherer

Yang Guo

(I)

The dimming moon o'er mist-veiled town and water looms.
The beauty in orchid boat sings her dream.
I oft remember our meeting on silk-washing stream.
Now severed by three rivers long,
In vain through clouds into the azure sky I gaze.
Smiling, the beauty says,
"Our hearts are like the lotus blooms:
Their root may snap, their fibres join like my song."

（二）

采莲湖上棹船回，

风约①湘裙翠。

一曲琵琶数行泪，

望君归，

芙蓉开尽无消息。

晚凉多少，

红鸳白鹭，

何处不双飞！

① 约：轻微的。

(II)

Having gathered the lotus on the lake, she rows

On homeward way, her green skirt ripples when wind blows.

A song of pipa brings down tear on tear;

In vain she waits for her lord to appear.

Now lotus blooms all faded, he is not in sight.

How many lovebirds red and egrets white

She sees in the cool evening sky!

Nowhere but in pairs will they fly.

干荷叶①

刘秉忠

(一)

干荷叶,
色苍苍②,
老柄③风摇荡。
减了清香,
越添黄。
都因昨夜一场霜,
寂寞在秋江上。

① 干荷叶:曲牌名,是刘秉忠的自度曲,又名"翠盘秋"。
② 苍苍:深青色。
③ 老柄:枯黄的柄。

Tune: Dried Lotus Leaves

Liu Bingzhong

(I)

Lotus leaves dried
In color turned from green to grey,
Old stems in the wind sway.
With fragrance lost, they are in yellow dyed.
Last night frost chilled their dream.
They look now lonely on the autumn stream.

（二）

干荷叶，
色无多，
不耐风霜锉①。
贴秋波②，
倒枝柯③。
宫娃④齐唱《采莲歌》，
梦里繁华过。

① 锉：摧折。
② 贴秋波：倒伏在水面上。
③ 枝柯：荷叶的枝干。
④ 宫娃：本义指宫女，这里指采莲女。

(II)

Dried lotus leaves

Whose color grieves,

Can't bear the bite of hoary frost.

On autumn waves they're lost

With their stems broken.

The palace maids awoken

Sing songs of lotus gathered on the stream,

Whose prime is passed in dream.

（三）

南高峰，

北高峰，

惨淡烟霞洞①。

宋高宗②，

一场空。

吴山依旧酒旗风，

两度江南梦③。

---

① 南高峰、北高峰、烟霞洞：地名，均位于今浙江省杭州市。
② 宋高宗：南宋的第一个皇帝赵构。
③ 两度江南梦：五代吴越国和南宋曾先后建都于杭州，最终都败亡了。

(III)

Southern Peak high,
Northern Peak high,
The Cave of Rainbow Clouds utter a dreary sigh.
The Song Emperor High
In vain has now gone by.
On Southern Hills the wineshop streamers fly
Still as of yore,
But the thriving days of Song are no more.

耍孩儿
庄家不识构阑①

杜仁杰

（一）

风调雨顺民安乐，

都不似俺庄家快活。

桑蚕五谷十分收②，

官司无甚差科③。

当村许下还心愿，

来到城中买些纸火④。

正打街头过，

见吊个花碌碌纸榜⑤，

不似那答儿闹穰穰⑥人多。

---

① 构阑：宋元时演出戏剧和各种技艺的场所。
② 十分收：十足的收成，指丰收。
③ 差科：承担差役和缴纳租税。
④ 纸火：拜神用的纸钱、香烛等。
⑤ 花碌碌纸榜：指戏剧演出的海报。花碌碌指写满了字，或颜色鲜艳。
⑥ 闹穰穰：热闹纷乱的样子。

Tune: Teasing the Child

A Peasant Knows Not the Theatre

Du Renjie

(I)

People live happy when in time blows wind and falls rain,

But as we peasants none's so cheerful and gay

In bumper year of mulberry and grain

When no official disturbs us everyday.

My vow fulfilled, I should perform the rural rite,

So I go downtown to buy incense and candles bright.

As I pass by the fair,

I see colored ads hanging there.

Nowhere have I seen a more noisy crowd, nowhere!

（二）六煞

见一个人手撑着椽①做的门，

高声的叫"请请！"

道"迟来的满了无处停坐"。

说道"前截儿院本《调风月》②，

背后么末敷演《刘耍和》③"。

高声叫："赶散易得，

难得的妆哈④"。

---

① 椽：本指屋梁上承瓦片的木条，这里指勾栏门上的横梁。
② 院本《调风月》：院本，金元时期以滑稽、歌舞为主要内容的戏剧表演形式。《调风月》是当时经常演出的剧本。风月指男女之情。
③ 《刘耍和》：《录鬼簿》记载高文秀有杂剧《黑旋风附演刘耍和》，剧本已逸。
④ 赶散易得，难得的妆哈：赶场的散乐，即各处游行演出的小戏班的演出容易碰上，而勾栏里的正规演出却是非常难得。妆哈：亦作"妆喝"，意为捧场、喝彩。

(II) The Last But Six

I see a man keeping the gate open with one hand,
Crying loud: "Come in please, please!"
Late, you'll find the house full and nowhere to sit but stand.
First, actors will perform the Moon and Breeze,
And then the play of an actor wellknown to this land.
"It's easy to find a place to enjoy and pause,
But hard to win your hearty applause."

（三）五煞

要了二百钱放过咱，

入得门上个木坡①。

见层层叠叠团圞②坐。

抬头觑是个钟楼模样③，

往下觑却是人旋窝④。

见几个妇女⑤向台儿上坐。

又不是迎神赛社⑥，

不住的擂鼓筛锣。

---

① 木坡：指观众坐的木阶梯看台。
② 圞：圆形。
③ 钟楼模样：指戏台。
④ 旋窝：指观众非常拥挤，就像水的漩涡一样。
⑤ 几个妇女：指为戏剧伴奏的女艺人，她们坐在前台中间靠后的位置上。
⑥ 赛社：民间风俗，农事完毕之后，用酒食祭祀土地神，然后农民饮酒庆祝。社：土地神。

(III) The Last But Five

I pay two hundred coins and I'm let in.

I enter, mount a wooden slope and hear a din.

I see an amphitheatre with seats in tier.

Looking up, I see a towerlike stage appear;

Looking down, I find the crowd like a whirlpool,

And women musicians sitting on the stool.

It is not a sacred procession long.

Why do I hear without cease drum and gong?

（四）四煞

一个女孩儿转了几遭，

不多时引出一伙。

中间里一个央人货。

裹着枚皂头巾

顶门上插一管笔①，

满脸石灰

更着些黑道儿抹。

知他待是如何过？

浑身上下，

则穿领花布直裰②。

---

① 顶门上插一管笔：指戏剧演员的头饰上竖着高高的翎毛，像一支笔。
② 直裰：长袍。

(IV) The Last But Four

For several rounds a maiden comes forth and back,

Then she leads a group of four from the rear.

Among them there's a villain clown,

Whose head is wrapped in a hood black,

With a brush on the ear;

Whose face with lime is white,

Streaked with paint black as night.

What will he do?

From top to toe

He wears a motley gown.

（五）三煞

念了会诗共词，
说了会赋与歌。
无差错。
唇天口地无高下①，
巧语花言记许多。
临绝末②，
道了低头撮③脚，
爨④罢将幺拨。

---

① 唇天口地无高下：指嘴皮子很厉害。
② 临绝末：到了最后。
③ 撮：收回。
④ 爨：宋代杂剧和金代院本中开头时都有一小段演唱，演唱内容多为滑稽调笑，也叫艳段。

(V) The Last But Three

He reads some verse

And sings some song,

There's nothing wrong.

Who knows which's better and which worse?

I only remember many words sweet.

What at the end is said?

He bends his head and keeps close his feet.

After the prelude, the melodrama will be played.

（六）二煞

一个妆做张太公,
他改做小二哥。
行行行说①向城中过。
见个年少的妇女
向帘儿下立,
那老子用意铺谋
待取②做老婆。
教小二哥相说合,
但要的豆谷米麦,
问甚布绢纱罗。

---

① 行行行说：边走边说。
② 取：通"娶"。

(VI) The Last But Two

One actor plays the role of grandpa old,
Another acts the waiter of a wine shop.
They walk and talk of life,
And at the central place they stop,
Seeing a young woman standing under the screen.
The grandpa covets her as wife,
And asks the waiter to be go-between,
How much grain, rice, peas and wheat
She wants as dowry and how many feet
Of cloth, silk, satin and brocade, all told.

（七）一煞

教太公往前挪①，

不敢往后挪，

抬左脚不敢抬右脚。

翻来覆去由他一个。

太公心下实焦躁，

把一个皮棒槌

则一下打做两半个。

我则道脑袋天灵破，

则道兴词告状，

划地②大笑呵呵。

① 挪：移动。
② 划地：平白地，莫名其妙地。

(VII) The Last But One

Told to go forward, ay!

The grandpa dare not backward go.

Told to raise his foot high,

He dare not put it low.

He turns back and forth as he is led,

Anxious at heart, he starts

And breaks the leather-wrapped hammer into two parts.

I mistake it for a broken head,

And fear they'll go to court after,

But unexpectedly I hear them burst in laughter.

（八）尾

则被一胞尿
爆①的我没奈何，
刚捱刚②忍更待看些儿个，
枉被这驴颓笑杀我③。

① 爆：涨，憋尿的意思。
② 刚：勉强。
③ 枉被这驴颓笑杀我：因为中途退场，看不到后面的精彩演出，被旁人取笑。驴颓：骂人的粗话。

(VIII) The Last Song or Epilogue

Hard pressed to pass water, I make for the door,
Though I try to hold it back so as to see more.
But how can I be set free?
I am afraid these sons of bitch will laugh at me.

醉中天

咏大蝴蝶①

王和卿

弹破庄周梦②,
两翅驾东风。
三百座名园、
一采一个空。
谁道③风流种,
唬杀④寻芳的蜜蜂。
轻轻飞动,
把卖花人搧⑤过桥东。

---

① 大蝴蝶:相传中统(1260—1264)年初,燕市(北京)有一只蝴蝶,巨大异常,王和卿于是作此曲。
② 庄周梦:战国时庄周梦见自己变成了一只蝴蝶。
③ 谁道:谁料。
④ 唬杀:吓坏。
⑤ 搧:摇动使生风。

Tune: A Drinker's Sky

Song of a Huge Butterfly

Wang Heqing

Breaking a philosopher's dream,
He flaps his wings and rides on the east wind in flight.
He gathers all the honey from the flowers
In three hundred well-known gardens and bowers.
Don't say the lover of beauty and breeze
Has scared away all honey-seeking bees!
Flapping his fan-like wings so light,
He blows the flower-seller off across the stream.

一半儿

题 情

王和卿

（一）

书来和泪怕开缄，

又不归来空再三。

这样病儿谁惯耽①！

越恁瘦岩岩②，

一半儿增添一半儿减③。

（二）

将来书信手拈着④，

灯下恣恣观觑⑤了。

两三行字真带草，

提起来越心焦，

一半儿丝挦一半儿烧⑥。

---

① 谁惯耽：谁能长久地忍受。
② 瘦岩岩：瘦弱的样子。
③ 一半儿增添一半儿减：增添了愁苦，减少了体重，而曲中并不说破，含蓄婉转。
④ 手拈着：紧握在手中。
⑤ 观觑：偷偷地看。
⑥ 一半儿丝挦一半儿烧：一边思量着，一边赶紧把信烧掉。丝：思。

Tune: Half and Half

Parting Grief

Wang Heqing

(I)

When I receive his letter, my tears rain;
I am afraid to open it, for again and again
He said he'd come back, but in vain.
How could I not grow thin and my grief be appeased?
When one half has decreased, the other has increased.

(II)

I take his letter near at hand,
And read it by lamplight carefully.
He wrote carelessly these two lines or three,
Which I am anxious to understand.
Half of his letter is torn apart,
Another half burns my heart.

（三）

别来宽褪缕金衣，
粉悴烟憔①减玉肌。
泪点儿只除衫袖知。
盼佳期，
一半儿才干一半儿湿。

① 粉悴烟憔：指面容憔悴。

(III)

My golden robe turns loose since my love from me parted;
My powdered face and jadelike skin look broken-hearted.
Tears dripping drop by drop only known to my sleeves, I
Wait for him with a sigh,
My sleeves are half wet and half dry.

小桃红

江岸水灯[1]

盍西村

万家灯火闹春桥[2],

十里光相照。

舞凤翔鸾[3]势绝妙。

可怜[4]宵!波间涌出蓬莱岛[5]。

香烟乱飘,

笙歌喧闹,

飞上玉楼[6]腰。

---

[1] 江岸水灯:盍西村所作"临川八景"中的第三首。描写的是元宵节江岸灯火与船上灯火交相呼应的热闹景象。
[2] 闹春桥:灯火把江上的桥装点得光芒四射、热闹惹眼。闹:热闹,惹眼。
[3] 舞凤翔鸾:形容各式各样的灯火表演。凤:凤形的灯。鸾:传说中凤凰一类的鸟,此处指鸾形的灯。
[4] 可怜:可爱。
[5] 蓬莱岛:相传是海上的仙山,这里比喻水上的灯船。
[6] 玉楼:相传是天帝的居所。

Tune: Red Peach Blossoms

(I) Lantern Lights on the River

He Xicun

Thousands of lanterns run riot on vernal shore,

Light overspreads for miles and miles.

Wonderful dancing phoenixes and dragons soar

Into the lovely night.

Out of the waves emerge three fairy isles.

See incence waft in flight;

Hear music on flute played!

They fly up around the tower of jade.

小桃红

客船晚烟

盍西村

绿云冉冉①锁清湾,

香彻②东西岸。

官课今年九分办③;

厮④追攀,

渡头买得新鱼雁⑤。

杯盘不干,

欢欣无限,

忘了大家难⑥。

---

① 绿云冉冉:烟雾笼罩的样子。
② 彻:香气浓烈。
③ 官课今年九分办:官家的课税今年只按九分征收。本曲写的是江干人家听说减税消息后的欢欣。
④ 厮:跟着,相互。
⑤ 新鱼雁:新鲜的鱼和雁,它们都是下酒的好菜。
⑥ 忘了大家难:大家一时忘了艰难的时光。

Tune: Red Peach Blossoms

(II) River Bay at Dusk

He Xicun

The clear bay is locked in clouds green-dyed;

Fragrance spreads to east and west riverside.

Only nine-tenths of taxes need to be paid this year.

How joyful people appear!

At the ferry they buy fresh fowls and fishes

To make plentiful dishes.

Their joy reaches its prime,

All forget the hard time.

小桃红

杂 咏

盍西村

杏花开候①不曾晴,

败尽游人兴。

红雪②飞来满芳径。

问春莺,

春莺无语风方定。

小蛮③有情,

夜凉人静,

唱彻醉翁亭。

---

① 候:时候。
② 红雪:飘落的杏花。
③ 小蛮:唐代诗人白居易有姬妾名小蛮,纤瘦美丽。后来,小蛮成为美貌歌姬的代称。

Tune: Red Peach Blossoms

(III) Mid-spring

He Xicun

Since apricots bloomed, the weather drear

Has disappointed the sightseer.

Blooms fall like red snow over the fragrant way.

I ask the oriole where is spring;

It answers not and the wind dies away.

Hear the young songstress sing

When all are still in the cool night!

Only she sings for the old drinker out of sight.

潘妃曲①

商 挺

带月披星担惊怕,

久立纱窗下。

等候他。

蓦②听得门外地皮儿踏,

则道是冤家③。

原来是风动荼蘼④架。

① 潘妃曲:曲调名,亦称"步步娇"。
② 蓦:突然。
③ 冤家:对心上人的昵称。
④ 荼蘼:一种藤本植物,夏季开花,香气袭人。

Tune: Song of Princess Pan

Shang Ting

Shivering with fright

In moonlight and starlight,

I stand long by the window dim,

Waiting for him.

Suddenly outdoor footsteps I seem to hear:

O it must be my dear.

But how again I shiver

To find in the wind only the trellis quiver.

沉醉东风

渔 樵

胡祗遹

渔得鱼①心满意足;
樵得樵②眼笑眉舒。
一个罢了钓竿,
一个收了斤斧③。
林泉下偶然相遇,
是两个不识字渔樵士大夫。
他两个笑加加④的谈今论古。

① 渔得鱼:渔夫捕到鱼。
② 樵得樵:樵夫砍到柴。
③ 斤斧:斧头。
④ 笑加加:笑呵呵。

Tune: Intoxicated in East Wind

Fisherman and Woodcutter

Hu Zhiyu

A fisherman is content with a basketful of fishes;
A woodcutter with a bundle of firewood he wishes.
One smiles on shouldering his fishing rod and line;
The other, with brows unknit, puts back his ax fine.
By chance they meet beside the fountain.
Though illiterate, they know much in the mountain.
Now and then they burst into laughter,
When they talk about the days before and after.

喜春来

伯 颜

金鱼玉带罗襕扣,
皂盖朱幡列五侯①。
山河判断在俺笔尖头②。
得意秋,
分破帝王忧③。

---

① 金鱼玉带罗襕扣,皂盖朱幡列五侯:作者服饰高贵,仪仗风华,可见自家的官位显赫。金鱼:指佩戴的金鱼符。玉带:镶嵌着金玉的腰带。罗襕:罗制的官服。皂盖:黑色的罗盖。朱幡:红色旗帜。五侯:公、侯、伯、子、男五等诸侯,这里泛指高官。
② 山河判断在俺笔尖头:指自己的地位举重若轻,有指点江山之大权。
③ 分破帝王忧:为帝王分忧解愁。

Tune: Welcome to Spring

Bo Yan

Adorned with gold fish and belt of jade,
I button my robe of brocade,
Under black canopy and banners red,
Of the five highest lords I'm at the head.
The land is ruled at the tip of my pen.
What pride over all men!
I bear my share of the imperial care.

平湖乐

尧庙^① 秋社

王 恽

社^② 坛烟淡散林鸦。

把酒观多稼^③。

霹雳弦声^④斗高下,

笑喧哗,

壤歌亭^⑤外山如画。

朝来致有西山爽气,

不羡日夕佳^⑥。

① 尧庙：在山西临汾城南三里。尧是我国古代传说中的贤明帝王，每逢丰收，人们就会去尧庙祭祀。
② 社：秋社，是立秋后的第五个戊日，这是古代祭祀土神、庆祝丰收的节日。
③ 多稼：丰收的庄稼。
④ 霹雳弦声：指拉弓射箭的声音。
⑤ 壤歌亭：古时临汾城外有击壤亭，相传是唐尧时老人击壤而歌的地方。
⑥ 朝来致有西山爽气，不羡日夕佳：指秋社的早晨，清爽宜人。

Tune: Joy of Calm Lake

Autumn Festival at Emperor Yao's Temple

Wang Yun

The incense on the altar fades

And crows disperse into the glades.

Wine cup in hand and bumper harvest in view,

I hear strings rumbling low and high,

Mingle with cheerful cry.

Beyond Labor Pavilion hills look like pictures fair.

At dawn the western hills exhale fresh air.

Why should I envy Southern Mountain hue?

节节高
题洞庭鹿角[①]庙壁

卢 挚

雨晴云散,
满江明月。
风微浪息,
扁舟一叶。
半夜心,
三生[②]梦,
万里别,
闷倚篷窗睡些[③]。

---

① 鹿角:洞庭湖畔有一鹿角镇。该曲是作者初别家乡亲人,赴湖南上任途经鹿角时所作的。
② 三生:佛教用语,指过去、现在、未来三生转世。指诗人心潮澎湃,思绪万千。
③ 睡些:小睡一会儿。

Tune: Higher and Higher

Written on the Temple Wall on Lake Dongting

Lu Zhi

After the rain clouds clear away;

Over the lake the moon sheds its ray.

The waves are calmed when the wind light

Blows on my leaflike boat at midnight.

In my heart deep,

Of my past life I dream.

I'll go far on the stream;

Depressed in the lonely boat, I get a short sleep.

沉醉东风

秋 景

卢 挚

挂绝壁枯松倒倚①,
落残霞孤鹜齐飞②。
四围不尽山,
一望无穷水。
散西风满天秋意。
夜静云帆月影低,
载我在潇湘③画里。

① 挂绝壁枯松倒倚：出自李白《蜀道难》："枯松倒挂倚绝壁。"
② 落残霞孤鹜齐飞：出自王勃《滕王阁序》："落霞与孤鹜齐飞，秋水共长天一色。"鹜：野鸭。
③ 潇湘：湘水发源于广西，在湖南与潇水汇合，成为"潇湘"，现称湘江。这里比喻湘江风景美如画。

Tune: Intoxicated in East Wind

(I) Autumn

Lu Zhi

The frowning cliff thrusts out a bending ancient pine;

With lonely swan fly rainbow clouds on the decline.

Surrounded by endless hill on hill,

On boundless water I gaze my fill.

The western breeze spreads autumn air in wide, wide skies.

The shadow of my cloudlike sail hangs low at moonrise.

My boat seems to float in the picture of two streams.

沉醉东风

闲 居

卢 挚

恰离了绿水青山那答,
早来到竹篱茅舍人家。
野花路畔开,
村酒槽头① 榨。
直吃的欠欠答答②。
醉了山童不劝咱,
白发上黄花乱插。

① 槽头:制酒的器具。
② 欠欠答答:迷迷糊糊,醉酒的样子。

Tune: Intoxicated in East Wind
(II) Rural Life

Lu Zhi

Having just left green hills and water blue,

I come to thatched cots with fence of bamboo.

By the roadside wild flowers blow;

In the trough I see home brew flow.

I eat till drunk I stagger along.

The lad won't care if I am wrong,

To wear yellow flowers on my white hair.

沉醉东风

春 情

卢 挚

残花酿蜂儿蜜脾,
细雨和燕子香泥。
白雪柳絮飞,
红雨桃花坠①。
杜鹃声又是春归。
纵有新诗赠别离,
医不可②相思病体。

---

① 白雪柳絮飞,红雨桃花坠:柳絮像白雪一样纷飞,桃花如红雨一般坠落。
② 医不可:医不好。

Tune: Intoxicated in East Wind

(III) Spring

Lu Zhi

Bees gather honey from lingering flowers;
Swallows build nest with clay wet with showers.
Willow down wafts like snow white,
Like rosy rain peach petals in flight.
The cuckoos sing the parting spring.
Though I write new verse when you part,
How can I cure you of your lovesick heart!

蟾宫曲

扬州汪右丞席上即事

卢　挚

江城①歌吹风流,

雨过平山,

月满西楼。

几许年华?

三生醉梦,

六月凉秋。

按锦瑟佳人劝酒,

卷珠帘齐按凉州②。

客去还留,

云树萧萧,

河汉悠悠。

① 江城：指扬州。
② 齐按凉州：一同演奏起了《凉州曲》。《凉州曲》即汉代乐府《凉州词》。

Tune: Song of Moon Palace

(I) At a Feast in the River Town

Lu Zhi

In river town songs are sung with the flowing breeze.
The rain has passed over plain and hill,
The western tower steeped in moonbeams.
How many years are gone with ease?
My life old and new drunk away in dreams,
The sixth moon foretells an autumn cool.
My wine cup filled by lustist beautiful,
Crimson curtain uprolled, I hear songs of frontier.
How can I not linger still?
Before me cloud-veiled trees shiver
Under the endless Heaven's River.

蟾宫曲

醉赠乐府朱帘秀

卢 挚

系行舟谁遣卿卿①？
爱林下风姿,
云外歌声。
宝髻堆云②,
冰弦散雨③,
总是才情。
恰绿树南熏晚晴,
险些儿羞杀啼莺。
客散邮误亭,
楚调将成,
醉梦初醒。

---

① 卿卿：旧时男女间的昵称。
② 宝髻堆云：你美丽的头发像云一样堆积。
③ 冰弦散雨：你用冰冷的琴弦弹奏出像雨点般灵动的乐曲。

Tune: Song of Moon Palace

(II) Written for My Fair Songstress While Drunk

Lu Zhi

Who sends you, my fair songstress, to my boat?

I love you come like breeze into the wood with ease.

Beyond the cloud your songs float.

I see your cloudlike hair

And hear your icy strings spread rain in the air,

In which I find a genius mind.

The south wind blows from green woods into evening sky.

Your songs would make warbling orioles feel shy.

When guests leave the post, I seem to be lost.

Awake from drunken dream,

I write this on the stream.

殿前欢

酒 兴

卢 挚

酒杯浓,

一葫芦春色醉山翁①,

一葫芦酒压花梢重。

随我奚童②,

葫芦干,

兴不穷。

谁人共?

一带青山送。

乘风列子③,

列子乘风。

---

① 山翁:山简,晋朝名士,镇守襄阳时,每天都饮酒大醉。
② 奚童:做杂役的小童。
③ 列子:列御寇,《庄子·逍遥游》说他可以"御风而行"。

Tune: Joy before Palace
Wine

Lu Zhi

Deep drunk,

In a gourd of spring hue I'm sunk.

A gourd of wine weighs down the tip of tree,

My page follows me.

My gourd is dried,

I'm still in spirits high.

Who will take a drink by my side?

A belt of green hills will not say goodbye.

On the wind I ride.

Who is riding, the wind or I?

山坡羊①

叹世

陈草庵

晨鸡初叫,
昏鸦争噪,
哪个不去红尘闹②?
路遥遥,
水迢迢,
功名尽在长安道。
今日少年明日老。
山依旧好,
人憔悴了。

---

① 山坡羊:曲调名,又称"山坡里羊""苏武持节"。
② 哪个不去红尘闹:人人都在追名逐利。红尘:世俗的名利世界。

Tune: Sheep on the Slope

O World

Chen Cao'an

At dawn cock crows;

At dusk caw crows.

Who to vanity fair is not eager to go?

Long long the way;

Far far the stream.

Only in the capital can you fullfill your dream.

Tomorrow old will grow the youth of today.

The hills are as green as before,

But the prime of youth is no more.

白鹤令

关汉卿

香焚金鸭鼎①,
闲傍小红楼。
月在柳梢头,
人约黄昏后。

① 金鸭鼎:鸭形的小香炉。

Tune: Song of White Crane

Guan Hanqing

Incense in golden censer burned,
I stand in red bower unconcerned.
The moon atop the willow tree,
At dusk my lover trysts with me.

四块玉

别　情

关汉卿

自送别,
心难舍,
一点相思几时绝?
凭阑袖拂梅花雪①。
溪又斜②,
山又遮,
人去也。

① 梅花雪:雪一般的梅花。
② 溪又斜:曲折的河溪。

Tune: Four Pieces of Jade

Parting Grief

Guan Hanqing

Since you are gone,

For you I long.

When will my yearning come to end?

I lean on rails, caressed by snow-like willow down.

The stream you went along

At hillside takes a bend.

It's screened from view

Together with you.

四块玉

闲 适

关汉卿

（一）

意马收，

心猿锁①，

跳出红尘恶②风波。

槐阴午梦③谁惊破？

离了利名场，

钻入安乐窝，

闲快活。

---

① 意马收，心猿锁：与世间种种烦恼决绝，表达了明显的归隐之意。
② 恶：险恶。
③ 槐阴午梦：用南柯梦的典故，唐传奇《南柯太守传》写书生到槐安国，娶了公主，做了南柯郡太守，显赫一时，后来被国王疏远，书生才发现一切不过是个梦，槐安国与南柯郡只是他庭前的两个蚁穴。

Tune: Four Pieces of Jade

Life of Easy Leisure

Guan Hanqing

(I)

Halt running horse and bind

Ape-like whimsical mind!

Leap out of a world which raves with dust and waves!

Wake up from noonday dream of glory vain!

Get rid of fame and gain!

Take a rest in your nest of pleasure

And enjoy your leisure!

（二）

南亩耕，

东山卧①，

世态人情经历多。

闲将往事思量过。

贤的是他，

愚的是我，

争什么②？

---

① 南亩耕，东山卧：意为将要归隐田园。陶渊明《归园田居》："开荒南亩际，守拙归原田。"
② 贤的是他，愚的是我，争什么：正话反说，愤慨于当时颠倒是非，不分贤愚的世态人情。

(II)

Having tilled the southern field, I
At the foot of eastern hill lie.
I've known the world and its ways,
And ponder at leisure the past days.
O wise is he
And foolish me!
What should I contend to be?

沉醉东风
送 别

关汉卿

咫尺的天南地北,
霎时间月缺花飞①。
手执着饯行杯,
眼阁②着别离泪。
刚道得声保重将息,
痛煞煞叫人舍不得。
好去者,
望前程万里!

① 咫尺的天南地北,霎时间月缺花飞:描写好友顷刻间天各一方,前一句从空间上说,后一句从时间上说,运用了夸张、象征等手法,耐人寻味。古人以"花好月圆"比喻男女美满地相聚,这里用"月缺花飞"比喻悲痛地分离。
② 阁:同"搁",意为含着。

Tune: Intoxicated in East Wind

Farewell Song

Guan Hanqing

We stand so near yet we'll be poles apart soon;

In a moment flowers will fall and wane the moon.

We hold in hand the farewell cup,

In our eyes tears well up.

I have just said, "Take care to keep fit!"

How painful is it

To tear myself away!

I can only say, "Go your way for the bright day!"

大德歌

关汉卿

（一）

谢家村，赏芳春。
疑怪他桃花冷笑人①。
着谁传芳信②？
强题诗也断魂，
花阴下等待无人问，
只听得黄犬吠柴门。

---

① 疑怪他桃花冷笑人：怀疑那些桃花在暗暗地嘲笑我。
② 芳信：指诗人牵挂之人的踪迹。

Tune: Song of Great Virtue

Guan Hanqing

(I)

In the Fair's Village lingering,
I seek the beauty of last spring.
I wonder if the peach blossoms laugh at me.
Who will tell me where is she?
I cannot force myself to write a verse.
My broken heart turns out worse.
In flowers' shade I have no one to ask but wait;
I only hear a dog bark at the wicket gate.

（二）

风飘飘，

雨潇潇，

便做陈抟①也睡不着。

懊恼伤怀抱。

扑簌簌泪点抛。

秋蝉儿噪罢寒蛩儿②叫。

淅零零细雨打芭蕉。

① 陈抟：北宋隐士，传说他可以一觉百余日而不醒。
② 寒蛩儿：蟋蟀。

(II)

The wind soughs hour after hour;

The rain falls shower by shower.

Even the Sleeping God cannot fall asleep.

Regret and sorrow hurt me deep,

My tears drip drop by drop,

After cicadas trill crickets chirp without stop.

It further grieves

To hear rain drizzle on banana leaves.

碧玉箫

关汉卿

（一）

膝上琴横，
哀愁动离情。
指下风生，
潇洒弄清音。
锁窗前月色明，
雕栏①外夜气清。
指法轻，
助起骚人②兴。
听！
玉漏③断，
人初静。

① 雕栏：雕花的栏杆。
② 骚人：诗人，指自己。
③ 玉漏：更漏，古代计时的器具。玉漏是对它的美称。

Tune: Green Jade Flute

Guan Hanqing

(I)

With zither on my knees,
I'm moved to think of my far-off dear.
My fingers play with ease
On zither strings a music clear.
Before my window screen the moon is bright;
Beyond the balustrade fresh is the night.
My touches light
Would make the poets' verve freer.
O Hear!
From water clock there comes no sound;
Silence begins to reign all around.

（二）

席上尊前，
衾①枕奈无缘。
柳底花边，
诗曲已多年。
向人前未敢言，
自心中祷苍天。
情意坚，每日空相见。
天！
甚时节成姻眷②？

① 衾：被子。
② 姻眷：结成眷属。

(II)

At the banquet, before a cup of wine,

Beside the flowers, beneath the willow,

For years I've sung and you've written verse fine.

But we've no chance to share the quilt and pillow.

What before others dare I say?

I can only in my heart pray.

Though our love firm remain,

Yet day by day we meet in vain.

Which day,

O Heaven, in our life

Can we be man and wife?

一枝花

关汉卿

（一）不伏老

攀出墙朵朵花，

折临路枝枝柳。

花攀红蕊嫩，

柳折翠条柔①。

浪子风流。

凭着我攀花折柳手，

直熬得②花残柳败休。

半生来折柳攀花，

一世里眠花卧柳。

---

① 攀出墙朵朵花，折临路枝枝柳。花攀红蕊嫩，柳折翠条柔：都是攀花折柳的意思，指在风月场中的风流生活。出墙花，指妓女。语出叶绍翁《游园不值》："春色满园关不住，一支红杏出墙来。"原无此意，但被后人借用。临路柳，也是指妓女。语出敦煌曲子词《望江南》："我是曲江临池柳，这人折了那人攀；恩爱一时间。"
② 直熬得：一直弄到。

Tune: A Sprig of Flowers

Guan Hanqing

(I) Don't Say I'm Old

I pluck flower on flower over the wall,
And break off branch on branch of willow tree.
The red pistil of the flower is tender;
The green twigs of the willow are slender.
A gallant like me
Will gather flowers and break off branches till I see
Withered leaves and flowers fall.
I have been picking them half my life;
I'll love and sleep with them as with a wife.

（二）梁州

我是个普天下郎君①领袖，
盖世界浪子班头②。
愿朱颜③不改常依旧，
花中消遣，
酒内忘忧；
分茶攧竹④，
打马藏阄⑤。
通五音六律滑熟⑥，
甚闲愁到我心头？

① 郎君：本指贵家子弟，有时也作妇女对丈夫或情人的称呼。元曲中一般指嫖客。
② 班头：领袖。
③ 朱颜：青春容颜。
④ 攧竹：一种赌博性的游戏。
⑤ 藏阄：古时的一种游戏。
⑥ 滑熟：熟练。

(II) Tune: The Frontier

I am the leading gallant under the sky,
And the most dissolute lover on earth.
I wish no face should lose its rosy dye.
I'd lead among flowers a life of mirth,
And drown my sorrow in wine;
I'd drink tea, and bet with bamboos,
Gamble on horse-race and in lottery.
There is no music but I can play a part.
How could sorrow come into my heart?

伴的是银筝女①银台前理银筝笑倚银屏②；

伴的是玉天仙③携玉手并玉肩同登玉楼；

伴的是金钗客歌金缕④捧金樽满泛金瓯。

你道我老也暂休。

占排场⑤风月功名首，

更玲珑又剔透⑥。

我是个锦阵花营都帅头⑦，

曾玩府游州⑧。

---

① 银筝女：弹奏银筝的歌女。筝：古代的一种弦乐器。银筝：装有银饰的筝。
② 银屏：银质的屏风。
③ 玉天仙：美貌的女子，这里指妓女。
④ 金缕：古曲调《金缕衣》的简称，这里指代歌曲。
⑤ 排场：娱乐场所。
⑥ 玲珑又剔透：灵活惯熟。
⑦ 都帅头：首领。
⑧ 玩府游州：在各州府闲荡游玩。

Who is in my company

But the lutist leaning on silver screen

And playing on silver lute in silver bower;

Hand in hand and side by side, the fairy queen

Going up with me to the jade tower;

The songstress adorned with golden hairpin,

Golden cup in hand, singing of golden dress and flower.

You say I'm old and should retire,

But in gallantry I'm going up higher and higher.

Growing more clever for ever and ever,

I'm winner in the camp of flowers,

Loafing from place to place, in golden bowers.

（三）隔尾

子弟每是个茅草岗

沙土窝初生的兔羔儿

乍向围场①上走。

我是个经笼罩受索网

苍翎毛老野鸡

踏踏②的阵马儿③熟。

经了些窝弓冷箭蜡枪头④，

不曾落人后。

恰不道⑤"人到中年万事休"，

我怎肯虚度了春秋？

---

① 围场：围猎之地，借指风月场。
② 踏踏：大步行走。
③ 阵马儿：战阵之马。
④ 窝弓冷箭蜡枪头：指风月场对客人的暗算。窝弓：装了机关，埋藏于山野的捕兽弓箭。冷箭：料不到的背后放箭。蜡枪头：蜡做的枪头，指好看而无实用的样子货。
⑤ 恰不道：岂不闻。道，听闻。

(III) Tune: The Interlude

The young gallants are new-born bucks in chase of bunny,

Coming out of the burrows in the mound,

And running for the first time on hunting ground.

I'm an old pheasant with feather grey,

Having escaped from traps and nets on the way,

And running like a steed

At fullest speed.

Nearly hit by spearheads and arrows from hidden bows,

Now I've reached middle age and known so many things,

How could I waste more autumns and springs?

（四）尾

我是个蒸不烂煮不熟

捶不匾①炒不爆

响珰珰一粒铜豌豆②。

恁子弟每谁教你钻入他

锄不断砍不下

解不开顿不脱

慢腾腾千层锦套头③？

我玩的是梁园月④，

饮的是东京⑤酒，

赏的是洛阳花⑥，

攀的是章台柳⑦。

---

① 匾：同"扁"。
② 铜豌豆：此处含有隐喻性格坚强的意思。
③ 锦套头：本义是套网，这里指妓女笼络客人的手段。
④ 梁园月：指代勾栏中的美色。
⑤ 东京：宋元时东京为汴州，即今开封。
⑥ 洛阳花：牡丹。这里借指名花。
⑦ 章台柳：美貌的妓女。章台，汉时长安章台下街名，旧时用为风月场所的代称。

(VI) Tune: Epilogue

I'm a resounding copper pea

Which could not be

Hammered out, cooked, fried or stewed.

How can you young gallants penetrate into me

Like a manifold harness which cannot be

Hoed up or cut down,

Slowly rid of or quickly hewed?

I have enjoyed in royal garden the moonshine,

In the east capital good wine,

And peony flowers in the west,

And plucked a twig from my lover's breast.

我也会吟诗,

会篆籀,

会弹丝。

会品竹,

我也会唱鹧鸪,

舞垂手,

会打围①,

会蹴鞠②,

会围棋,

会双陆。

你便是落了我牙,

歪了我口,

瘸了我腿,

折了我手,

天赐与我

---

① 打围:古代打猎的合围,后泛指打猎。
② 蹴鞠:古人踢球的一种游戏。

I'm good at poetry

And at calligraphy;

I can play on the string

And draw a picture of bamboo,

I can also sing

The songs of partridge too.

With hands hanging down I can dance,

In hunting I can advance,

I know how to play football and chess,

And I gamble by chance.

You may knock my teeth down

Or my mouth wry,

Even if you break

My leg and hand,

Though disabled am I,

这几般儿歹症候^①,
尚兀自^②不肯休。
则除是^③阎王亲自唤,
神鬼自来勾^④,
三魂归地府,
七魄丧冥幽^⑤,
天哪,那其间^⑥
才不向烟花路上走。

① 歹症候:坏毛病。
② 兀自:犹,还。
③ 则除是:只除是,除非是。则:只。
④ 勾:引。
⑤ 冥幽:地狱。
⑥ 那其间:那个时候。

Still firm I'll stand,

Unless

The Satanic Majesty

Or the demons come to summon me.

Even one-third of my soul goes to the hell

And two-thirds sink into the infernal well,

O Heaven, only then

Will I not go on the dark willowy lane.

寄生草

饮

白　朴

长醉后方何碍①?
不醒时有甚思②?
糟腌两个功名字,
醅渰千古兴亡事,
曲埋万丈虹霓志③。
不达时④皆笑屈原非;
但知音尽说陶潜是⑤。

① 碍:妨碍,挂碍。
② 有甚思:还有什么思念。
③ 糟腌两个功名字,醅渰千古兴亡事,曲埋万丈虹霓志:在痛饮大醉中忘掉功名、兴亡和壮志。糟腌:用酒糟腌制。醅渰:用浊酒淹没。曲埋:拿酒曲埋掉。
④ 不达时:不显达于时的人们。
⑤ 陶潜是:陶潜是对的,即他不满官场黑暗,走向归隐田园的路,是正确的。

Tune: Parasite Grass

Drinking

Bai Pu

What ails when I'm drunk long?
When I don't wake, what's wrong?
Let undying fame and glory be drowned in wine!
Forget the ups and downs of days gone by!
Bury in songs ambitions rainbow-high!
The unsuccessful laugh at Qu Yuan in water sunk,
While connoisseurs approve Tao Qian in wine drunk.

阳春曲①

题 情②

白 朴

轻拈斑管③书心事,
细折银笺写恨词。
可怜不惯害相思,
则被你个肯字儿
迤逗④我许多时。

① 阳春曲:曲牌名,一名"喜春来",中吕宫常用的曲调。
② 题情:原作六首,这里选录一首,此曲是第一首。
③ 斑管:毛笔笔管上的斑纹,这里借指毛笔。
④ 迤逗:挑逗,勾引。

Tune: Song of Spring
For My Love

Bai Pu

I take up my pen light stained with tears to write
My heart-felt grief and then I fold the paper white.
Alas! unused to lasting longing for a mate,
It takes me such a long, long time to wait
For your vain promise of a date.

天净沙①

白 朴

（一）春

春山暖日和风，
栏杆楼台帘栊②，
杨柳秋千院中。
啼莺舞燕，
小桥流水飞红③。

（二）夏

云收雨过波添，
楼高水冷瓜甜，
绿树阴垂画檐。
纱厨④藤簟，
玉人罗扇轻缣⑤。

---

① 天净沙：越调常用的曲牌名，一名"塞上秋"。
② 帘栊：窗帘。
③ 飞红：落花。
④ 纱厨：帐子，因为形状像厨而得名。
⑤ 玉人罗扇轻缣：美人手摇罗扇，身穿薄纱。

Tune: Sunny Sand

Bai Pu

(I) Spring

The sun and gentle breeze warm hills in spring,
The curtained bower girt with balustrade.
Among the willows in the garden hangs the swing.
The swallows dance and orioles sing
On running stream under the bridge fallen reds fade.

(II) Summer

Waves rise when clouds clear away with rain fleet;
By tower high water is cold and melon sweet.
Green willow leaves shade painted eaves.
On bamboo mat in curtained bed, she's fair as jade,
In silken dress with a fan of brocade.

（三）秋

孤村落日残霞，
轻烟老树寒鸦，
一点飞鸿①影下。
青山绿水，
白草红叶黄花。

（四）冬

一声画角谯门②，
半庭新月黄昏③，
雪里山前水滨。
竹篱茅舍，
淡烟衰草孤村。

---

① 飞鸿：大雁。
② 谯门：也作"樵门"，指建有瞭望楼的城门。
③ 黄昏：指新月颜色浅黄，不太明亮。

(III) Autumn

At sunset over lonely village rainbow clouds glow;
Over mist-veiled old trees flies a cold crow.
The shadow of a dot of swan in flight
Over green hills and bluish rills
Sees leaves red, flowers yellow and dewy grass white.

(IV) Winter

A dreary horn blows in watch-tower on city wall;
The crescent moon sheds twilight into half the hall;
The waterside and hillside are covered with snow.
A bamboo-fenced cottage only
Stands in the village lonely,
Where with a wreath of smoke wafts a cold crow.

沉醉东风

渔 夫

白 朴

黄芦①岸白蘋②渡口,
绿杨堤红蓼③滩头。
虽无刎颈交④,
却有忘机友⑤。
点秋江白鹭沙鸥,
傲煞人间万户侯⑥,
不识字烟波钓叟。

---

① 黄芦：枯黄的芦苇。
② 白蘋：一种水草。
③ 红蓼：水边的草，花为浅红色。
④ 刎颈交：至死不渝的友情。
⑤ 忘机友：忘却机心，淡泊超然的朋友。
⑥ 万户侯：汉代的封制，指达官显贵。

Tune: Intoxicated in East Wind

Fisherman

Bai Pu

The rivershore overgrown with yellow reed,
The ferry decorated with white duckweed,
The bank is shaded by willows green and the beach head
Adorned with knotweed red.
Although I have no life-long friends,
My companions conceive no evil ends.
The autumn river is dotted with gulls and herons white.
I look down on the lords proud of their might.
A fisherman old, I fish in mist and water cold.

醉高歌

感 怀

姚 燧

十年书剑长吁①,
一曲琵琶暗许②。
月明江上别湓浦③,
愁听兰舟夜雨。

① 十年书剑长吁:我一生都坎坷不得志。书剑:指文人生涯。长吁:长叹。
② 暗许:私下认同。
③ 湓浦:水名,今为开龙河,在江西省九江市西。

Tune: Drinking Song

Reflection

Yao Sui

I sigh after ten years with books and sword.
The lutist's song is a promise without word.
I leave the river town when the moon shines bright,
Afraid to hear rain in orchid boat at night.

凭阑人寄征衣

寄征衣①

姚 燧

欲寄君衣君不还,
不寄君衣君又寒。
寄与不寄间,
妾身千万难。

① 征衣:远行者的寒衣。

Tune: Leaning on Balustrade

The Winter Garment

Yao Sui

If I send winter garment to thee,

Thou wilt not come to the household.

If I do not, thou wilt feel cold.

It is hard to decide for me

If I should send it to thee.

雁儿落过得胜令

庾天赐

（一）雁儿落

从他绿鬓斑，
欹枕白石烂。
回头红日晚，
满目青山矸①。

（二）得胜令

翠立数峰寒，
碧锁暮云间②。
媚景春前赏，
晴岚雨后看③。
开颜，
玉盏金波满。
狼山，
人生相会难。

---

① 从他绿鬓斑，欹枕白石烂。回头红日晚，满目青山矸：指人生匆匆，转眼之间，少年变成了老年，倚靠的白石烂了，回首间太阳落山了，满眼的青山都要粉碎了。
② 翠立数峰寒，碧锁暮云间：写早春的景色，青翠的山峰矗立在天外寒气中，暮云在山腰缠绕着。
③ 媚景春前赏，晴岚雨后看：明媚的春光要及时观赏，山上的云雾要赶在雨后观看，不能错失机会。

From "Falling Swan" to "Triumphant Song"

Yu Tianci

(I) Tune: Falling Swan

Let my black hair turn grey!
I'll pillow my head on white stone till its decay.
I turn my head: the setting sun reddens the sky;
Verdant hills look serene to the eye.

(II) Tune: Triumphant Song

Peak on peak stands like emerald;
Cloud on cloud locks the evening cold.
Gaze on the charming vernal plain
And sun-lit hills after the rain!
O brighten up
And fill to the brim with golden wine the jade cup!
Deep in the hill,
It's hard for us to meet, so let's enjoy our fill!

黑漆弩

村居遣兴

刘敏中

长巾阔领①深村住,
不识我唤作伧父②。
掩白沙翠竹柴门,
听彻③秋来夜雨。
闲将得失思量,
往事水流东去。
便宜教画却凌烟④,
甚是功名了⑤处?

① 长巾阔领:指自己粗俗的打扮。
② 伧父:鄙夫,粗野的农夫。
③ 彻:完,全部。
④ 凌烟:指凌烟阁,是皇帝图画功臣、表彰他们的地方。
⑤ 了:了却,尽头。

Tune: Varnished Black Bow

Written at Random in the Village

Liu Minzhong

Wearing long hood and large collar in my cot,
I'm called a rude fellow by those who know me not.
My wicket gate closed to bamboos green and sand white,
I listen to the rain throughout the autumn night.
Pondering at leisure gain and loss, weal and woe,
I see the past like running water eastward flow.
Even if my portrait should in high tower remain,
Is it the end of glory I try to attain?

四块玉

浔阳江①

马致远

送客时,

秋江冷,

商女琵琶断肠声。

可知道司马②和愁听?

月又明,酒又酲③。

客乍醒。

① 浔阳江:本曲取材于白居易《琵琶行》,借写白居易在浔阳江遇见琵琶女一事,来抒发自己的"天涯沦落人"之感。
② 司马:州官的副职,在唐朝时已成闲差,这里是指白居易。
③ 酲:酒醒后困倦疲惫得如同生病的状态。

Tune: Four Pieces of Jade

(I) On River Xunyang

Ma Zhiyuan

When we two part,

The autumn river is cold.

The lutist's song would break our heart.

Don't you know Poet Bai of old

Who listened to the lute with heart-break?

The moon's as bright;

We're drunken quite,

But soon we wake.

四块玉

叹 世

马致远

两鬓皤①,中年过,
因甚区区②苦张罗?
人间宠辱都参破。
种春风二顷田,
远红尘千丈波③,
倒大来④闲快活。

① 皤:白。
② 区区:同"驱驱",奔走忙碌之意。
③ 千丈波:比喻巨大的风险。
④ 倒大来:到头来。

Tune: Four Pieces of Jade
(II) O World!

Ma Zhiyuan

Grey turns my hair

Past middle age.

Why should I be busy about worldly affair?

I've seen through fame and shame as a sage.

I'd till in vernal breeze two acres of land;

Far from the world's ups and downs I would stand.

What a great pleasure

To live at leisure!

天净沙

秋 思

马致远

枯藤老树昏鸦,
小桥流水人家,
古道西风瘦马。
夕阳西下,
断肠人①在天涯。

① 断肠人:漂泊天涯、极度忧伤的人。

Tune: Sunny Sand

Autumn Thoughts

Ma Zhiyuan

Over old trees wreathed with rotten vines fly crows;

Under a small bridge beside a cot a stream flows;

On ancient road in western breeze a lean horse goes.

Westwards declines the setting sun.

Far, far from home is the heart-broken one.

清江引①

野 兴

马致远

（一）

绿蓑衣②紫罗袍③谁是主？

两件儿都无济。

便作钓鱼人，

也在风波里。

则不如寻个稳便处闲坐地。

（二）

林泉隐居谁到此？

有客清风至④。

会作山中相⑤，

不管人间事。

争什么半张名利纸？

① 清江引：曲调名，又名"江水儿"。
② 绿蓑衣：比喻渔人或隐士。
③ 紫罗袍：比喻入仕做官。
④ 有客清风至：唯有清风似客来。
⑤ 山中相：南朝陶景弘起初任齐朝将军，齐亡之后，他隐居茅山不愿出仕。梁武帝每有国家大事，无不去信请教，时人称陶景弘为"山中宰相"。后人常常以"山中宰相"比喻隐士。

Tune: Song of Clear River

Rural Pleasure

Ma Zhiyuan

(I)

Green straw cloak and violet silken gown,
Which is up? Which is down?
Neither will do. Even a fisherman
Should avoid perilous waves if he can.
I'd seek a safe place as I please
To sit with ease.

(II)

Who'd come to my hermitage amid the trees?
My only guest is the fresh breeze.
Living by the fountain,
I'm minister in the mountain.
I do not care for worldly affair.
Why should I strive to enter the vanity fair?

寿阳曲①

马致远

(一) 山市晴岚②

花村外,
草店西,
晚霞明雨收天霁。
四围山一竿残照里,
锦屏风又添铺翠。

(二) 远浦帆归

夕阳下,
酒旆③闲,
两三航未曾着岸。
落花水香茅舍晚,
断桥头卖鱼人散。

---

① 寿阳曲:曲调名,又名"落梅风"。
② 晴岚:雨后晴空中清新的雾气。
③ 酒旆:酒店的旗帜。

Tune: Song of Long-lived Sun

Ma Zhiyuan

(I) The Sun-lit Mist-veiled Mountain

By blooming village-side,

West of the shop of wine,

Rainbow clouds after rain brighten the sky far and wide.

The surrounding hills steeped in sinking sunshine,

The embroidered screen is again paved with emerald green.

(II) The Returning Sails

The sun sinks behind the hill,

The wineshop's streamer's still.

Two or three fishing boats have not yet come ashore.

Fallen petals sweeten water before the door.

By the end of the day

Fish-sellers disperse on homeward way.

（三）潇湘夜雨

渔灯暗①，
客梦回②，
一声声滴人心碎。
孤舟五更家万里，
是离人几行情泪。

---

① 渔灯暗：夜晚的江面被一片雨雾笼罩着，远处渔船上的灯火也显得昏暗了。
② 梦回：梦醒。

(III) Night Rain on the River

Dim fishers' lanternlight,
I wake up from my dream.
The rain drips drop by drop to break my heart.
My lonely boat is far from home deep in the night.
It rains as tears which stream
Down from the eyes of those who part.

夜行船[1]

马致远

（一）秋思

百岁光阴一梦蝶[2]，

重回首往事堪嗟[3]。

今日春来，

明朝花谢。

急罚盏夜阑[4]灯灭。

（二）乔木查

想秦宫汉阙[5]，

都做了衰草牛羊野。

不恁么渔樵[6]没话说。

纵荒坟横断碑，

不辨龙蛇[7]。

---

[1] 夜行船：曲牌名。
[2] 梦蝶：借用"庄周梦蝶"的典故，比喻浮生如梦。
[3] 堪嗟：可叹。
[4] 夜阑：夜深。
[5] 秦宫汉阙：秦汉时的宫殿。
[6] 渔樵：打鱼的人和砍柴的人，指代隐者。
[7] 龙蛇：龙年、蛇年，指年份。意谓断碑上所刻的那些字都辨认不清了，同时也隐喻圣贤豪杰与凡夫俗子同归荒野，功过莫辨了。

Night-sailing Boat

Ma Zhiyuan

(I) Tune: Autumn Thoughts

Like a dream pass a hundred years of light and shade;
Turning my head, I sigh for days gone by.
Spring comes today, tomorrow flowers fade.
Drink the cup dry
Before lamplight goes out at dead of night!

(II) Tune: The Arbor

I think of ancient palaces, alas!
They become pastures covered with withered grass.
Of the fishermen's gossip they are aliments,
Crisscrossed with ruined tombs and broken monuments,
On which dragons and snakes are blent.

(三)庆宣和

投至狐踪与兔穴①,

多少豪杰!

鼎足②虽坚半腰里折。

魏耶?

晋耶?

(四)落梅风

天教你富,

莫太奢!

没多时好天良夜。

富家儿更做道③你心似铁,

争辜负了锦堂风月④!

---

① 投至:乃至。狐踪与兔穴:狐兔出没的地方,指荒野。
② 鼎足:指魏、蜀、吴三国的并立。
③ 更做道:即使,纵然。
④ 争:相当于怎。锦堂风月:指高雅脱俗、轻富贵薄虚誉的生活。

(III) Tune: Celebration of the Reign

I find fox's traces and hare's holes.

Where are the ancient heroes' souls?

Like a tripod's broken legs the three states are not strong.

To which succeeding dynasty did the empire belong?

(IV) Tune: Falling Mume Blossoms

No matter how rich you may be,

Don't live in luxury!

O happy days and nights cannot forever last.

No matter how hard a miser's heart may be,

The breezy moonlit days will soon be past!

（五）风入松

眼前红日又西斜，

疾似下坡车。

不争镜里添白雪①，

上床与鞋履相别。

休笑巢鸠计拙②，

葫芦提③一向装呆。

（六）拨不断

名利竭，

是非绝。

红尘④不向门前惹。

绿树偏宜屋角遮，

青山争补墙头缺。

更那堪竹篱茅舍！

① 白雪：白发。
② 巢鸠计拙：相传斑鸠不会筑巢。
③ 葫芦提：糊涂。
④ 红尘：尘土，世俗社会。

(V) Tune: The Wind through Pines

The setting sun goes west before the eye

As quickly as the carriage rolling down the height.

Don't let your hair in the mirror turn snow-white!

Go to bed and say to your shoes goodbye!

Don't laugh at the cuckoo occupying the magpie's nest!

Play the fool like a gourd and take your rest!

(VI) Tune: Unbroken String

In the vanity fair

There is no right nor wrong.

No dust is raised before my door all the day long,

The eaves of my roof is shaded by trees green,

My broken wall seems crowned with hills like a screen.

What's more, I've my bamboo-fenced cot in evening air!

（七）离亭宴煞

蛩①吟罢一觉才宁贴，

鸡鸣时万事无休歇，

争名利何时是彻！

看密匝匝蚁排兵，

乱纷纷蜂酿蜜，

急攘攘蝇争血。

裴公绿野堂②，

陶令③白莲社。

爱秋来时那些：

和露摘黄花④，

带霜分紫蟹，

煮酒烧红叶。

---

① 蛩：蟋蟀。
② 裴公绿野堂：《旧唐书·裴度传》载，唐宪宗时裴度累官至中书侍郎，后来退居洛阳，筑绿野堂，与白居易等饮酒吟咏其中。
③ 陶令：曾为彭泽县令的陶渊明。
④ 黄花：菊花。

(VII) Tune: Feast at Farewell Pavilion

When crickets sing,

I can sleep well.

At cockcrow everything

Begins to stir up.

When will end the strife

For fame and gain?

See ants surround their prey in flood,

Bees gather honey pellmell,

And flies hasten to suck blood.

I would retire to the green plain

Or at the foot of White Lotus Hill.

I love, when autumn is chill,

To pluck golden flowers inpearled with dew,

To eat frost-proof crabs with you,

And to burn red leaves to heat wine.

想人生有限杯,
浑几个重阳节。
嘱咐你个顽童记者①:
便北海探吾来,
道东篱醉了也②。

① 者:"着",语助词。
② 便北海探吾来,道东篱醉了也:不管谁来,都说我醉了不能相见。北海,指代后汉时曾为北海相的孔融,据《后汉书·孔融传》载,他曾自称只要座上客常满,樽中酒不空,自己便无忧了。

How many cups can we drink in our life?

How many can we enjoy mountain-climbing days fine?

I ask my lad to tell any guest

That I am taking my rest

At my eastern hedge with my wine cup!

寿阳曲

马致远

从别后,
音信绝,
薄情种害煞人也,
逢一个见一个因话说,
不信你耳轮儿不热①。

① 不信你耳轮儿不热:民间认为,被人念叨会耳朵发热。

Tune: Song of Long-lived Sun

Ma Zhiyuan

Since thou left me,

I have received no word from thee.

Such unkindness has injured me.

I complain to whoever appears.

I don't believe it won't assail thy ears.

后庭花

秋 思

赵孟頫

清溪一叶舟,
芙蓉①两岸秋。
采菱谁家女?
歌声起暮鸥②。
乱云愁,满头风雨,
戴荷叶归去休③。

① 芙蓉:荷花的别名。
② 歌声起暮鸥:化用宋代李清照《如梦令》:"常记西亭日暮,沉醉不知归路,兴尽晚回舟,误入藕花深处,争渡,争渡,惊起一滩鸥鹭。"
③ 休:语气词,相当于"吧"。

Tune: Backyard Flowers

Autumn Thoughts

Zhao Mengfu

On the clear stream she rows a leaf-like boat,

Lotus blooms spread autumn hue to the shore.

Who is gathering lotus seed, at dusk afloat?

She startles gulls with her folklore.

From gloomy clouds grief is shed,

Wind and rain overspread,

She goes back with a lotus leaf over her head.

十二月过尧民歌[①]

别　情

王实甫

（一）十二月

自别后遥山隐隐，更那堪远水粼粼？
见杨柳飞绵滚滚，对桃花醉脸醺醺。
透内阁[②]香风阵阵，掩重门暮雨纷纷。

（二）尧民歌

怕黄昏不觉又黄昏；
不销魂怎地不销魂？
新啼痕压旧啼痕；
断肠人忆断肠人。
今春，
香肌瘦几分；
搂带[③]宽三寸。

---

① 十二月过尧民歌：这是一支带过曲，由同属于一个宫调的《十二月》和《尧民歌》组成。
② 内阁：闺阁。
③ 搂带：缕带，束腰的带子。

From "A Year's End" to "Folklore"

Parting Grief

Wang Shifu

(I) Tune: A Years's End

Since we parted, far-flung hills disappear with you.
How can I bear to see the rippling stream anew,
And wave on wave of willow catkin's wafting trace,
And peach blossom's drunken face before my face?
The fragrant breeze invades my bower now and then;
Evening rain falls on my closed door again and again.

(II) Tune: Folklore

The dim twilight I fear will often reappear.
O how can my soul lost be found at any cost?
The new cannot efface the old tear-shedding trace;
One broken heart yearns for the other kept apart.
When spring sets in,
Fragrant as is my skin,
My girdle turns loose for my waist grows thin.

普天乐

滕 宾

翠荷残,
苍梧坠①。
千山应瘦,
万木皆稀。
蜗角名,
蝇头利,
输与渊明陶陶醉。
尽黄菊围绕东篱,
良田数顷,
黄牛一只,
归去来兮!

① 苍梧坠:青翠的梧桐叶坠落了。

Tune: Universal Joy

Teng Bin

Lotus blooms fade,

Green plane leaves fall.

Hills on hills appear lean;

Woods on woods cast less shade.

Of what avail

Are the fame and gains small

Like the horn of a snail

Or the head of a fly green?

Why not get drunk with the poet in his east bower,

Among chrysanthemums in flower,

Why not till with plough in hand

A few acres of land

With your yellow buffalo?

Why don't you homeward go?

叨叨令

道 情

邓玉宾

白云深处青山下,
茅庵草舍无冬夏。
闲来几句渔樵话①,
困来一枕葫芦架。
你省的也么哥②?
你省的也么哥?
煞强如风波③千丈
担惊怕。

① 渔樵话:与渔夫和樵夫闲谈。
② 也么哥:语助词,无意义。
③ 风波:指险恶的世道。

Tune: Chattering Song

At Leisure

Deng Yubin

Deep in the mountain under the clouds white,

In thatched cot I fear nor summer nor winter night.

At leisure I talk with woodcutter and fishermen;

Drowsy, I sleep 'neath trellis of gourds now and then.

Do you not know,

Do you not know?

It's better than to rest in anxiety and fright

On waves high and low.

叨叨令

道　情

邓玉宾

一个空皮囊
包裹着千重气①；
一个干骷髅
顶戴着十分罪②。
为儿女使尽些拖刀计③，
为家私费尽些担山力。
你省④的也么哥，
你省的也么哥？
这一个长生道理何人会？

---

① 千重气：古人认为人活一口气，气绝就是死去。
② 顶戴着十分罪：经受了各种磨难。
③ 拖刀计：使人上当受骗的伎俩。
④ 省：醒悟。

Tune: Chattering Song

O World

Deng Yubin

Nothing but air

Is enveloped in your skin;

Your dry bones bear

Nothing but sin on sin.

For your children you may do right or wrong;

You'd shoulder mountains a fortune to win.

Do you understand my song?

Do you understand my song?

Do nothing silly if you want to live long!

殿前欢

懒云窝①

阿利西瑛

懒云窝,
醒时诗酒醉时歌。
瑶琴不理抛书卧,
无梦南柯②。
得清闲尽快活。
日月似撺梭过,
富贵比花开落。
青春去也,
不乐如何?

---

① 懒云窝:作者的居所,在今江苏苏州。
② 无梦南柯:不做荣华富贵的梦。

Tune: Joy before Palace

My Nest for Idle Cloud

Ali Xiying

In my Nest for Idle Cloud,

Sober, I drink and write; while drunk, I croon aloud.

I will not read nor on lute will I play,

Nor dream to climb up high.

I will make merry at leisure,

And let sun and moon like shuttles pass by.

Wealth and rank, after all,

Like flowers, will bloom and fall.

The prime of youth has passed away.

What should I do if not seek pleasure?

鹦鹉曲

山亭逸兴

冯子振

嵯峨①峰顶移家住,
是个不唧溜②樵父。
烂柯③时树老无花,
叶叶枝枝风雨。
故人曾唤我归来,
却道不如休去。
指门前万叠云山,
是不费青蚨④买处。

① 嵯峨:高绝险峻。
② 唧溜:机灵。
③ 烂柯:传说晋人王质入山砍柴,见童子下棋就丢下斧子去观看。等到他起身离去的时候,发现斧柄已经烂掉了。回家一问,才知道已经过去十年了。柯:斧头柄。
④ 青蚨:钱的别称。

Tune: Song of Parrot

A Hermit's Pleasure in the Mountain Pavilion

Feng Zizhen

I move my house atop the frowning hill;

As a woodman I am a green hand still.

I play chess till flowers fall from old trees,

Branch on branch, leaf on leaf, in rain and breeze.

My friends would call me back, but I say

I'd rather stay.

Pointing to clouds and hills before my door,

I need not pay for the scene I adore.

鹦鹉曲

别　意

冯子振

花骢嘶断留侬①住,
满酌酒劝据鞍父②。
柳青青万里初程,
点染阳关朝雨。
怨春风雁不回头,
一个个背人飞去。
望河桥敛衽③悲啼,
早蓦到长亭短处。

① 侬:你。
② 据鞍父:骑马即将离去的男子。
③ 衽:衣襟,衣袖。

Tune: Song of Parrot

Parting Grief

Feng Zizhen

Your dappled horse neighs when I ask you to stay.

I fill your cup with wine to detain you in vain.

The green willows will see you go far, far away

To see the Sunny Pass dotted with morning rain.

I complain why, without turning the head, the wild geese

Should fly away one by one with the vernal breeze.

Gazing on the bridge, I wipe with my sleeves tear on tear.

Soon I find the Pavilion of Adieu is near.

寿阳曲

答卢疏斋①

朱帘秀

山无数,

烟万缕,

憔悴煞玉堂人物②。

倚篷窗③一身儿活受苦。

恨不得随大江东去④。

---

① 卢疏斋:卢挚,号疏斋。
② 玉堂人物:指翰林学士卢挚,玉堂为翰林院别称。
③ 篷窗:船窗。
④ 恨不得大江东去:指恨不能尽快了结此生。

Tune: Song of Long-lived Sun

Reply to Lu Zhi

Zhu Lianxiu

O countless mountains

And wreaths of smoke!

Languid becomes the man in broidered cloak.

I lean on the casement like heart-broken fountains.

O could I be released with the waves going east!

塞鸿秋

代人作

贯云石

战西风几点宾鸿[①]至,
感起我南朝[②]千古伤心事。
展花笺[③]欲写几句知心事,
空教我停霜毫[④]半晌无才思。
往常得兴时,
一扫无瑕疵[⑤]。
今日个病厌厌
刚写下两个相思字。

---

① 宾鸿:大雁。
② 南朝:指宋、齐、梁、陈四朝。
③ 花笺:精美华丽的信纸。
④ 霜毫:一种白兔毛做成的毛笔。
⑤ 瑕疵:白玉上的斑点,这里指诗文中的小毛病。

Tune: Autumn Swan on Frontier

Written for a Friend

Guan Yunshi

In the west breeze shiver a few dots of wild geese.

It breaks my heart to think of the Southern Dynasties.

I spread out paper fine to write down heart-felt line.

Without inspiration, I put down my pen.

When I was in the mood to write then,

I would wipe all stains away.

How can I be so sick at heart today

As to write only two words I would forget:

"Everlasting regret".

红绣鞋

贯云石

挨着靠着云窗同坐,
偎着抱着月枕双歌。
听着数着愁着怕着
早四更过。
四更过情未足,
情未足夜如梭①。
天哪,
更闰②一更儿妨甚么!

① 夜如梭:夜晚很快就过去了。
② 闰:添,增加。

Tune: Embroidered Red Shoes

Guan Yunshi

To you I cling, on you I lean,

We sit side by side by the window-screen.

I snuggle up to you and into your embrace,

We sing against the pillow face to face.

I listen, count, worry and fear night will soon pass.

Night passed, but love is not alleyed, alas!

Love not alleyed, time flies away.

O Heaven, why don't you lengthen night into day!

落梅风

贯云石

新秋至,
人乍别,
顺长江水流残月①。
悠悠画船东去也,
这思量起头儿一夜。

---

① 顺长江水流残月:看着弯月顺着长江流走,暗指诗人一夜无寐,思念辗转。

Tune: Wind of Falling Mume Blossoms

Guan Yunshi

When comes the autumn new,

We have just parted.

Along the endless river floats the moon broken-hearted.

The eastward-going painted ship has bid adieu.

This is only the first night I'm longing for you.

蟾宫曲

送 春

贯云石

问东君①何处天涯?

落日啼鹃,

流水桃花,

淡淡遥山,

萋萋芳草,

隐隐残霞。

随柳絮吹归那答②,

趁游丝③惹在谁家?

倦理琵琶,

人倚秋千,

月照窗纱。

① 东君：思春之神，指春天。
② 那答：那里。
③ 游丝：春日里随风飘动的蛛丝。

Tune: Song of Moon Palace

Parting Spring

Guan Yunshi

I ask the Eastern God where's the end of the sky.

At sunset cuckoos cry,

On running water fall peach blooms,

Dim, dim distant hills loom,

Sweet grass seems filled with gloom,

Rainbow clouds thick with fumes.

Where is the willow down blown away by the breeze?

In whose house floats gossamer over the trees?

Tired of playing on the lute's string,

I lean against the swing.

The moon shines on my window screen.

清江引

咏 梅

贯云石

南枝夜来先破蕊,

泄露春消息。

偏宜雪月交,

不惹蜂蝶戏①。

有时节暗香来梦里。

---

① 偏宜雪月交,不惹蜂蝶戏:指梅花恰好开放在风雪交加的寒冬,不像其他的花一样招蜂引蝶,暗喻高雅的品格。

Tune: Song of Clear River

The Mume Blossoms

Guan Yunshi

The southern branches of mume trees

At night are the first to blow,

Revealing vernal beams.

They love the company of moon and snow,

But will not play with butterflies or bees.

Sometimes their gloomy fragrance steals into our dreams.

得胜令

四月一日喜雨

张养浩

万象①欲焦枯,
一雨足沾濡②。
天地回生意③,
风雨起壮图④。
农夫,舞破蓑衣绿,
和余欢喜的无是处。

① 万象:自然界的一切景物。
② 沾濡:滋润,润湿。
③ 生意:生机。
④ 壮图:人们对未来又充满希望。

Tune: Triumphant Song

Happy Rain on the First Day of the Fourth Moon

Zhang Yanghao

All plants wither and dry,

Rain falls to wet the earth.

All revive 'neath the sky;

The wind and cloud bring mirth.

The peasants dance

In wornout cloak of bamboo.

I'm happy in a trance,

Knowing not what to do.

水仙子

张养浩

中年才过便休官,
合共①神仙一样看。
出门来山水相留恋,
倒大来②耳根清眼界宽,
须寻思这的③是真欢。
黄金带缠着忧患,
紫罗襕裹着祸端④。
怎如俺藜杖藤冠⑤?

① 合共:总是。
② 倒大来:元曲习语,十分,非常。
③ 的:确实,实在。
④ 黄金带缠着忧患,紫罗襕裹着祸端:指官海无常。
⑤ 藜杖藤冠:指隐居生活。

Tune: Song of Daffodils

Zhang Yanghao

I am retired when I've just passed mid-age;
As paradise I look on my hermitage.
How lovely hills and rills outdoors appear!
There's nothing to offend the eye and ear.
It is true joy to think over and understand:
A golden belt may gird you with distress;
Woe may be hidden in violet official dress.
Why not wear a ratten cap, cane in hand?

山坡羊①

潼关怀古

张养浩

峰峦如聚,

波涛如怒,

山河表里②潼关路。

望西都③,

意踟蹰④。

伤心秦汉经行处⑤,

宫阙⑥万间都做了土。

兴,

百姓苦;

亡,

百姓苦。

① 山坡羊:曲牌名,又名"山坡里羊""苏武执节"。
② 表里:内外。
③ 西都:指长安。
④ 踟蹰:犹豫不决,徘徊不前。此处指思潮起伏,陷入沉思。
⑤ 伤心秦汉经行处:经过秦汉故地,内心伤感。
⑥ 宫阙:皇宫。

Tune: Sheep on the Slope

Thinking of the Past on My Way to Tong Pass

Zhang Yanghao

Peaks like brows knit,

Angry waves spit.

With mountain and river far and near,

On the road to Tong Pass I appear.

Gazing on Western Capital,

I hesitate, alas!

To see the place where ancient warriors did pass

The ancient palaces, hall on hall,

Are turned to dust, one and all.

Before my eyes,

The empirc's rise

Is people's woe;

The empire's fall

Is also people's woe.

朝天子[①]

张养浩

柳堤,

竹溪,

日影筛金翠[②]。

杖藜徐步近钓矶,

看鸥鹭闲游戏。

农夫渔翁,

贪营活计,

不知他在图画里。

对这般景致,

坐的,

便无酒也令人醉。

[①] 朝天子:曲调名,又名"朝天曲""谒金门"。
[②] 日影筛金翠:耀眼的阳光从树顶上照下来,形成金色和绿色斑驳的光影。

Tune: Skyward Song

Zhang Yanghao

Willowy shores,

Bamboo-lined stream,

The sun sieves green and golden shades as in a dream.

Cane in hand, slowly I go to the fishing place

To watch at leisure

Gulls and herons play with pleasure.

Peasants at the plough and fishermen on the oars

Do not know they are in a picture fine.

If with such a scenery you sit face to face,

You will get drunk without wine.

鹦鹉曲①

白 贲

侬家鹦鹉洲②边住,
是个不识字渔父。
浪花中一叶扁舟,
睡煞江南烟雨,
觉来时③满眼青山,
抖擞绿蓑归去。
算从前错怨天公,
甚④也有安排我处。

① 鹦鹉曲:又名"黑漆弩"。
② 鹦鹉洲:地名,位于湖北汉阳西南的长江上。
③ 觉来时:醒来时。
④ 甚:真,正。

Tune: Song of Parrot

Bai Ben

Living at Parrot Islet as I can,

I am an illiterate fisherman.

My leaflike boat braves the perilous waves.

I've slept through Southern rain and smoke.

My eyes are filled with green mountains when awake;

I come back, shaking water off my green straw cloak.

In bygone days I blame Heaven by mistake.

See how well he disposes me!

蟾宫曲

郑光祖

（一）

弊裘尘土压征鞍，

鞭倦袅芦花①。

弓剑萧萧②，

一竟入烟霞③。

动羁怀④

西风禾黍秋水蒹葭⑤。

千点万点老树寒鸦，

三行两行写高寒⑥

呀呀雁落平沙。

---

① 弊裘尘土压征鞍，鞭倦袅芦花：马上的游子衣衫破烂，满身尘土，连马鞭子都懒得举了。
② 萧萧：萧条。
③ 烟霞：荒野。
④ 羁怀：游子的情怀。
⑤ 蒹葭：芦苇。
⑥ 写高寒：高寒指萧瑟的天空，大雁排成"一"字或者"人"字形飞过，像在天空上写字。

Tune: Song of Moon Palace

Zheng Guangzu

(I)

My saddle laden with dust and outworn sable coat,

I wield my tired whip where reed catkins float.

Shivering with my sword and bow,

Straight into mist-veiled rainbow-clouds I go.

It moves a roamer's heart

To see the wheat undulate in the western breeze

And hear the reed rustle by the stream clear.

A thousand dots of cold crows on old trees,

Two or three rows of cawing wild geese

Fly through cold air and fall on the sand.

（二）

曲岸西边近水涡
鱼网纶竿钓艖①。
断桥东下傍溪沙
疏篱茅舍人家。
见满山满谷，
红叶黄花。
正是凄凉时候，
离人又在天涯②。

① 艖：船。
② 天涯：远方。

(II)

West of the winding shore near the whirlpool
Fishermen cast their net or fish with rod and line.
East of the dim bridge by the sand fine
A few bamboo-thatched cottages stand.
All over hills and vales full
Of red leaves and flowers in yellow dye.
In such a season sad and drear,
From home I'm far apart
At the end of the sky.

闺中闻杜鹃

曾 瑞

（一）骂玉郎

无情杜宇①闲淘气，
头直上②耳根底，
声声聒③得人心碎。
你怎知我就里④，
愁无际?

① 杜宇：杜鹃。
② 头直上：头顶上。
③ 聒：吵闹。
④ 就里：内心的思想感情。

Hearing the Cuckoo in My Boudoir

Zeng Rui

(I) Tune: Blaming My Gallant

How pitiless is naughty cuckoo's cry!
It has assailed my ears from on high.
Cry on cry has vexed me and broken my heart.
O cuckoo, how could you know the reason why
I feel a boundless grief to be kept apart!

（二）感皇恩

帘幕低垂，
重门深闭。
曲栏边，
雕檐外，
画楼西。
把春醒①唤起，
将晓梦惊回。
无明夜，
闲聒噪，
厮禁持②。

---

① 春醒：指春天人容易困倦的样子。
② 禁持：折磨，纠缠。

(II) Tune: Gratitude to the Emperor

The curtain hanging low,

Tightly closed double door,

The winding balustrade

And the sculptured eaves fade.

West of the painted bower you sing,

Awakening me, drunk in spring,

From my morning dream.

Do you not know

I cannot stand, night and day, any more

Your vexations like a stream?

（三）采茶歌

我几曾离
这绣罗帏?
没来由劝我道
"不如归①"！
江南正着迷,
这声儿
好去对俺那人啼。

---

① 不如归：古代传说，蜀王杜宇死后化作杜鹃鸟，鸣声悲切，就像在说："不如归去。"

(III) Tune: Tea-picking Song

O When have I

Left the embroidered screen?

Why should you cry

To me: "Better go home!"

My gallant in the south is entranced in love scene.

Why don't you cry to him not to roam?

集贤宾

曾 瑞

（一）宫词

闷登楼倚阑干
看暮景，
天阔水云平。
浸池面楼台倒影，
书云笺雁字斜横①。
衰柳拂月户云窗，
残荷临水阁凉亭。
景凄凉助人愁越逞②，
下妆楼步月空庭。
鸟惊环佩响，
鹤吹铎铃鸣。

---

① 书云笺雁字斜横：比喻大雁在空中排成"一"字形，或"人"字形飞过，就像以云天为信笺写字。
② 越逞：愈加厉害。

Tune: Meeting of Good Friends

Zeng Rui

(I) Palace Grief

Gloomy, I mount the tower, lean on the balustrade
And view the evening scene:
The sky is wide, clouds blend with water green.
The shadow of the bower drowned in the pool,
The wild geese write slanting words on clouds white.
The withered willow trees caress windows and door;
The lotus fades before waterside pavilions cool.
The dreary scene adds to my grief without words.
Going down, I pace in courtyard steeped in moonlight.
My ringing pendants startle the birds,
The crane cries and echo the bells of jade.

（二）逍遥乐

对景如青鸾舞镜①,

天隔羊车②,

人囚凤城③。

好姻缘辜负了今生,

痛伤悲雨泪如倾。

心如醉满怀何日醒?

西风传玉漏丁宁④。

恰过半夜,

胜似三秋,

才交四更。

---

① 对景如青鸾舞镜：意谓对景生悲。青鸾舞镜，南朝刘敬叔《异苑》记载，有位王侯得到一只鸾，为它装饰起金玉，准备了佳肴，它却三年不鸣。夫人提议，拿一面镜子来，让鸾以为看到同类，这样它也许会鸣叫。谁知，鸾看了镜中的影子，悲鸣不已，很快就死去了。
② 天隔羊车：意谓得不到皇帝的宠幸。羊车，史书记载晋武帝常乘坐羊车，任其在后宫行走，羊车停在哪里，他就在哪里歇宿。
③ 凤城：指京城。据传，秦穆公的女儿弄玉吹箫引凤至京城，所以凤城、丹凤城就成了京城的别称。
④ 丁宁：拟声词，形容水滴的声音。

(II) Tune: Joy to be Free

Seeing the gloomy scene, I'm sad as phoenix green.

From heaven I'm kept far apart

As if imprisoned in the phoenix town.

Could I have a happy marriage with my mate?

I'm so much grieved that tears like rain stream down.

Drunk with brimming cups, when will wake my heart?

I hear the water clock of jade stop

Dripping in the western breeze drop by drop.

Midnight just passed away,

It is colder than autumn late.

O when will break the day?

（三）金菊香

秋虫夜语不堪听,
啼树宫鸦不住声。
入孤帏强眠寻梦境,
被相思鬼绰①了魂灵,
纵有梦也难成。

（四）醋葫芦

睡不着,
坐不宁,
又不疼不痛病萦萦。
待不思量霎儿②
心未肯,
没乱③到更阑人静。

---

① 绰:夺走。
② 霎儿:一霎时,一会儿。
③ 没乱:烦躁。

(III) Tune: Fragrance of Golden Chrysanthemum

How can I stand

The autumn crickets' chirping shrill,

And crows in palace trees cawing still?

Going to lonely bed, how can I sleep?

My soul is seized by Lovesickness deep.

How can I go to the dreamland?

(IV) Tune: A Gourd of Vinegar

I cannot fall asleep

Nor sit with ease till deep

In the night I remain

Heartily sick without physical pain.

My heart will not consent

To my stifling awhile my lovesick sentiment.

（五）高平煞

照愁人残蜡碧荧荧，

沉水烟消金兽鼎①。

败叶走庭除②，

修竹扫苍楹③。

唱道是④人和闷可难争。

则我瘦身躯

怎敢共愁肠竞？

伤心情脉脉，

病体困腾腾⑤。

画屋⑥风轻，

翠被寒增，

也温不过早来袜儿冷。

① 金兽鼎：筑有兽形装饰的铜鼎。
② 除：台阶。
③ 苍楹：青色的堂前柱子，此处代指堂前。
④ 唱道是：实在是。唱：通"畅"。
⑤ 腾腾：指很严重的样子。
⑥ 画屋：有彩饰的精致房屋。

(V) Tune: High Level Epilogue

The green flame of the flickering candlelight grieves

The incense burned up in the censer of gold.

In the courtyard run riot withered leaves,

The pale pillars caressed by bamboos tall.

Can it be true that woman can fight the gloom?

Can I resist dreariness, lean as I loom?

Laden with grief, I am heart-broken;

Drowsy and sick, when can I be awoken?

Though the wind is light in the painted hall,

My green quilt is still cold.

How can it warm up my stockings at all?

（六）尾

睡魔盼不来，
丫环叫不应，
香消烛灭冷清清。
唯嫦娥与人无世情，
可怜咱孤零①。
透疏帘斜照月偏明。

① 孤零：孤单。

(VI) Tune: Epilogue

Sleep will not come to me at all;

My maid will not answer my call.

Incense burned up, lights out, I feel chill, sad and drear.

Only the sympathetic Moon Goddess

Pities my loneliness.

She sheds through my window screen slanting moonlight clear.

哨遍

睢景臣

（一）高祖①还乡

社长排门告示②，
但有的差使无推故。
这差使不寻俗③：
一壁厢④纳草除根，
一边又要差夫，
索应付。
又言是车驾，
都说是銮舆，
今日还乡故。
王乡老执定瓦台盘⑤，
赵忙郎⑥抱着酒葫芦。
新刷来的头巾，
恰糨来的绸衫，
畅好是妆幺大户⑦。

① 高祖：汉代开国皇帝刘邦的庙号。庙号是皇帝死后在太庙立室奉祀时特起的名号。
② 社长：社为基层单位。元代五十家为一社，推选长者为社长。告示：通知。
③ 寻俗：寻常，平常。
④ 一壁厢：一边，一面。
⑤ 乡老：乡间德高望重的长者。瓦台盘：陶制的托盘。
⑥ 赵忙郎：作者随意命名的农民。
⑦ 畅好是：真是。妆幺：装模作样的。大户：财主。

Tune: Whistling Around

Ju Jingchen

(I) The Emperor's Home-coming

The village chief announces from door to door:
Whatever errand no one should refuse to run.
The errand's not an ordinary one:
Rootless fodder be collected on the one hand;
On the other messengers should meet the demand.
Hard to deal with! They say.
The royal cortege will come
With the emperor to his home Today.
The village elder holds an earthen plate,
The busy young man a gourd of wine.
They wear the hood washed of late
And stiffened silk shirt fine.
All play the rich though they are poor.

（二）耍孩儿

瞎王留①引定火②乔③男女，

胡踢蹬④吹笛擂鼓。

见一彪⑤人马到庄门，

匹头里几面旗舒。

一面旗白胡阑⑥

套住个迎霜兔，

一面旗红曲连

打着个毕月乌⑦。

一面旗鸡学舞⑧；

一面旗狗生双翅⑨；

一面旗蛇缠葫芦⑩。

① 王留：元代农村泛称人名。
② 火：通"夥"，一帮。
③ 乔：装模作样，有丑陋浅薄之意。
④ 胡踢蹬：作者随意命名的农民。
⑤ 一彪：一队，一群。
⑥ 胡阑：合音为"环"，这里指月亮。此句是写月旗。
⑦ 曲连：合音为"圈"，这里指太阳。毕月乌，乌鸦。此句是写日旗。
⑧ 鸡学舞：舞凤旗。鸡：凤。
⑨ 狗生双翅：飞虎旗。狗：虎。
⑩ 蛇缠葫芦：蟠龙戏珠旗。蛇：龙。葫芦：珠。

(II) Tune: Playing the Child

A blind man leads men and women in strange array,

Pellmell they beat the drum and on flute they play.

See a troop of horsemen

Arrive at the gate then,

And at their head

Many banners outspread:

On the moon flag a frosty hare in a ring white,

On the sun flag a golden crow in crimson light,

On the wind flag a cock dances and sings,

On the tiger flag there's a dog with two wings,

On the dragon flag you will find

A snake around a gourd wind.

（三）五煞

红漆了叉，

银铮①了斧，

甜瓜苦瓜黄金镀②。

明晃晃马镫③枪尖上挑，

白雪雪鹅毛扇上铺。

这几个乔人物，

拿着些不曾见的器仗，

穿着些大作怪④衣服。

---

① 铮：镀。
② 甜瓜苦瓜黄金镀：指仪仗中的金瓜锤。
③ 马镫：仪仗中的朝天镫。镫：同"镫"。
④ 大作怪：稀奇古怪。

(III) Tune: Last Stanza But Five

Fork painted red,

Axe silver-white,

Melonlike hammer and spearhead

With stirrup bright

And plume fan white like snow,

These flag-bearers forward go,

Holding unknown staffs in a mess

And wearing motley dress.

（四）四煞

辕条①上都是马，
套顶②上不见驴，
黄罗伞柄天生曲③。
车前八个天曹判④，
车后若干递送夫⑤。
更几个多娇女⑥，
一般穿着，
一样妆梳。

① 辕条：车辕，车前驾牲口用的两根长木。
② 套顶：套在牲口脖子上的圈套及拉车的绳索。
③ 黄罗伞柄天生曲：帝王仪仗中的"曲盖"，柄弯曲，形状类似一把伞。
④ 天曹判：天上的判官，指皇帝车前导驾的侍臣，言其面无表情。
⑤ 递送夫：为皇帝拿物品，随时递送的侍臣或太监。
⑥ 多娇女：美女，指宫娥。

(IV) Tune: Last Stanza But Four

In the shafts steed on steed,

In harness there's no ass.

A crooked pole supports a yellow canopy.

Before the carriage eight officials lead;

Behind follow attendants in livery

And charming maid and lass

In the same dress,

With hair in tress.

(五)三煞

那大汉下的车,
众人施礼数①。
那大汉觑②得人如无物。
众乡老展脚舒腰拜,
那大汉挪身着手扶。
猛可里③抬头觑,
觑多时认得,
险④气破我胸脯。

① 施礼数:行礼。礼数:礼节。
② 觑:看。
③ 猛可里:猛然间。可里:助音词,无意义。
④ 险:差点儿。

(V) Tune: Last Stanza But Three

From the carriage a big fellow comes down,

Saluted by all the people from the town.

That fellow seems not to see those who kowtow.

With legs apart the village elders deeply bow,

To help them up that fellow forward goes.

Suddenly I look up who knows!

And gaze at him for long.

My breast nearly bursts with anger strong.

（六）二煞

你身须①姓刘,

你妻须姓吕②。

把你两家儿根脚③从头数。

你本身做亭长④耽几盏酒,

你丈人教村学读几卷书。

曾在俺庄东住,

也曾与我喂牛切草,

拽坝⑤扶锄。

① 须：本来。
② 吕：刘邦皇后姓吕。
③ 根脚：根底，出身底细。
④ 亭长：秦代十里为一亭，十亭为乡。亭设长，刘邦做过泗上亭长。
⑤ 拽坝：拉坝，坝即"耙"，一种碎土农具。

(VI) Tune: Last Stanza But Two

Your name is Liu,

Your wife is Lü.

I know the root of your family tree.

Fond of wine, you were chief around ten Ii.

Your father-in-law taught children to read.

You lived east of my farm to feed

Cattle for me and cut fodder for the cow

And till the land with the plow.

（七）一煞

春采①了桑，

冬借了俺粟。

零支②了米麦无重数。

换田契强称了麻三秤③，

还酒债偷量了豆几斛④。

有甚胡涂处？

明标着册历⑤，

现放着文书⑥。

① 采：指偷采。
② 零支：零借。
③ 秤：量词，十五斤为一秤。
④ 斛：一种量具。
⑤ 册历：账簿。
⑥ 文书：这里指借据。

(VII) Tune: Last Stanza But One

In spring you gathered mulberry,

In winter you borrowed millet from me.

You bought on credit countless rice and wheat.

Renewing contract, you took more hemp by cheat;

Paying your debt, you stole more beans and peas.

Why should you play the fool, please?

It's registered in account book.

If you do not believe, just take a look!

（八）尾声

少我的钱，差发①内旋拨还，

欠我的粟，税粮中私准除②。

只道刘三③，

谁肯把你揪捽④住？

白甚么⑤改了姓更了名，

唤做汉高祖！

① 差发：公差，元代被派的官差可以出钱替代。
② 私准除：暗中扣除。准：折合，相抵。
③ 刘三：刘老三，刘邦排行老三。
④ 揪捽：揪住，拽住。
⑤ 白甚么：为什么，有嘲讽之意。

(VIII) Tune: The Epilogue

You should at once pay the money you owed me,

And reduce the taxes on my millet and pea.

I only tell you, Liu the Third,

Holding you tight, I won't release you on your word.

Why should you change your name,

And steal an emperor's fame?

叨叨令

悲 秋

周文质

叮叮当当铁马儿乞留玎琅①闹,
啾啾唧唧促织儿依柔依然叫。
滴滴点点细雨儿渐零渐留哨②,
潇潇洒洒梧叶儿失流疏剌落。
睡不着也末哥,
睡不着也末哥,
孤孤零零单枕上迷丢模登③靠。

① 乞留玎琅:拟声词。下文的"依柔依然""渐零渐留""失流疏剌"均为拟声词。
② 哨:鸟叫。
③ 迷丢模登:迷迷糊糊。

Tune: Chattering Song

Grief in Autumn

Zhou Wenzhi

The iron bell on bell on the eave rings pellmell;
The crickets chirp so shrill chills my heart still.
Drizzling rain drips and drops but never stops;
Plane leaves fall in shower from hour to hour.
Alas! How could I fall asleep?
Alas! How could I fall asleep
Alone on lonely pillow when night is deep!

塞儿令

周文质

挑短檠①,
倚云屏②,
伤心伴人清瘦影。
薄酒初醒,
好梦难成,
斜月为谁明?
闷恹恹听彻残更,
意迟迟盼杀多情。
西风穿户冷,
檐马③隔帘鸣。
叮,
疑是佩环声。

① 短檠:矮灯架,这里指灯。
② 云屏:画有云的屏风,或指云母制成的屏风。
③ 檐马:系在屋檐下的铁片。

Tune: Song of Frontier

Zhou Wenzhi

Turning up candlelight,

Standing by cloudy screen,

Heart-broken, I'm accompanied by shadow lean.

Awakened from thin wine,

For vain sweet dreams I pine.

Why should the slanting moon be bright?

I'm gloomy and depressed all through the night.

How lovesick I'm for you who won't come here!

The west wind blowing through the door brings me chill.

Iron bells ring across the curtain still.

O hear!

Is it the pendants of my dear?

清江引

有　感

乔　吉

相思瘦因人间阻①,
只隔墙儿住。
笔尖和露珠,
花瓣题诗句,
倩②衔泥燕儿将③过去。

① 间阻:阻挡,作梗。
② 倩:请。
③ 将:捎,带。

Tune: Song of Clear River

Reflection

Qiao Ji

I grow so lean for I think of you hard,

Though only by a wall we're barred.

I use as ink dewdrops which drip

From my pen-tip

To write a verse on the petal of flower

And ask the swallow to send it to your bower.

清江引

即 景

乔 吉

垂杨翠丝千万缕,
惹住闲情绪①。
和泪送春归②,
倩水将愁去,
是溪边落红昨夜雨。

---

① 闲情绪:惜春之情。
② 和泪送春归:惜春之情与眼泪一起送春归去。

Tune: Song of Clear River

Vernal View

Qiao Ji

Thousands of emerald branches of willows weep

For they're grieved not to keep

Late spring from going.

In tears they bid adieu to water flowing

With grief-laden fallen red

Last night's riverside shower shed.

山坡羊

冬日写怀

乔 吉

（一）

朝三暮四①，

昨非今是。

痴儿不解荣枯事②。

攒家私，

宠花枝③，

黄金壮起荒淫志，

千百锭买张招状纸④。

身，已至此，

心，犹未死。

---

① 朝三暮四：指形势变幻反复无常。
② 荣枯事：荣华之后接着往往就是枯槁。
③ 花枝：指美丽的姬妾。
④ 千百锭买张招状纸：千百锭银钱最后只买一张招状纸。招状纸：古代犯人招认罪状的纸。意谓贪财好色的人最后的下场都是进监狱。

Tune: Sheep on the Slope

Thoughts in Winter

Qiao Ji

(I)

You change along,

Take right for wrong,

Too foolish to know weal from woe.

With fortune made,

You love fair maid.

Gold only props you up to wanton time;

Wealth piled up only leads to crime.

Body in jail,

Heart will not wail.

（二）

离家一月，

闲居客舍，

孟尝君不费黄韭社①。

世情别，

故交绝，

床头金尽谁行借？

今日又逢冬至节。

酒，何处赊？

梅，何处折？

---

① 孟尝君不费黄韭社：意谓我从哪里能得到免费的饭食啊？孟尝君：战国四公子之一，不惜重金招揽天下贤才，有门客数千。黄韭：指金子。

(II)

For a month I've left home,

Lodge in hospice and roam.

Where can I get a frugal meal without pay?

Shunning society,

Without old company,

From whom can I borrow when I've spent my gold?

Again it's winter solstice today.

Where's wine on credit sold?

Where's mume against the cold?

（三）

冬寒前后，

雪晴时候，

谁人相伴梅花瘦？

钓鳌舟，

缆汀洲，

绿蓑不耐风霜透。

投至①有鱼来上钩，

风，吹破头，

霜，皴②破手。

---

① 投至：等到。
② 皴：皮肤开裂，这里指被风霜冻裂的。

(III)

In winter day

Snow melts away.

Who is accompanying mume blossoms lean?

I moor my boat

And fish afloat.

The frosty wind has pierced my straw cloak green.

When fish comes to my hook, O look!

My head bitten by breeze,

My hands, frost-wrinkled, freeze.

卖花声

愤世

乔吉

肝肠百炼炉间铁,

富贵三更枕上蝶,

功名两字酒中蛇①。

尖风薄雪②,

残杯冷炙③,

掩青灯竹篱茅舍。

---

① 肝肠百炼炉间铁,富贵三更枕上蝶,功名两字酒中蛇:意谓我的心思像钢铁一样坚定,富贵于我就像梦中的蝴蝶,功名于我如同杯弓蛇影,它们都是那么虚无缥缈,丝毫不能让我动心。
② 薄雪:急雪。
③ 炙:烤熟的肉食。

Tune: Song of a Flower Seller
O World

Qiao Ji

My hardened heart's like iron in the stove,

Wealth and rank like butterfly once dreamed of,

Glory and fame but shadows in wine-cup.

Sharp wind and snowflakes down and up,

Cold meal left o'er,

In dimly-lit bamboo-fenced cot I shut the door.

凭阑人

乔 吉

(一) 春思

淡月梨花曲槛①旁,
清露苍苔罗袜凉。
恨他愁断肠,
为他烧夜香。

(二) 小姬

手拈红牙②花满头,
爱唱春词不解愁。
一声出画楼,
晓莺无奈羞。

---

① 槛:栏杆,围栏。
② 红牙:红牙板,古时歌姬唱歌时打节拍伴奏的乐器。

Tune: Leaning on Balustrade

Qiao Ji

(I) Yearning in Spring

Under pale moon by pear blossoms on rails I lean,
My silken stockings cold with clear dew on moss green.
Grief-stricken, I am in sad plight,
Still I burn incense for him at night.

(II) A Young Songstress

With flowers over the head and clappers in hand,
Singing spring songs, of grief she does not understand.
From painted bower her song streaks the sky.
How could the morning orioles not feel shy?

(三）金陵道中

瘦马驮诗天一涯，
倦鸟呼愁村数家。
扑头飞柳花，
与人添鬓华①。

---

① 鬓华：两鬓的白发。

(III) On My Way to Jinling

I roam on a lean horse laden with verse I write;

Tired birds bewail over desolate villages in sight.

Overhead willow down in flight

Adds to my forehead hair white.

折桂令

乔 吉

（一）毗陵晚眺

江南倦客①登临。

多少豪雄，

几许消沉。

今日何堪，

买田阳羡②，

挂剑长林③。

霞缕烂④谁家昼锦⑤，

月钩横故国丹心⑥。

窗影灯深，

磷火青青，

山鬼喑喑。

① 倦客：指仕宦不如意而隐退的人。
② 买田阳羡：宋代苏轼曾在《登州谢表》中写道："止求自便，买田阳羡，誓毕此身。"表达倦于官场沉浮，希望归田隐居的意愿。
③ 挂剑长林：晋代许逊曾为旌阳令，遇到晋室变乱，悟出世事皆虚，于是投身学道，最后修炼成仙。相传建昌县冷水观有一棵古松，曾是许逊遨游挂剑的地方。
④ 霞缕烂：霞光灿烂的早晨。
⑤ 昼锦：昼锦堂，相传为魏国公韩琦所建，富丽奢华。
⑥ 故国丹心：指失去了故国，成为前朝的遗民。

Tune: Plucking Laurel Branch

Qiao Ji

(I) Evening View

A tired roamer on southern shore,
I climb up high.
How many heroes sank of yore!
How can I bear to buy
Arable land and field
And hang my sword on the tree not to wield?
Whose house is steeped in brilliant sunset glow?
Whose heart is loyal as the hook-like moon hanging low?
Lamplight deep hidden behind the window screen,
I only see the phosphorus light green,
And hear the scream of ghost unseen.

（二）登毗陵永庆阁

忽飞来南浦①娇云，

背影藏羞，

忍笑含颦。

绕鬟兰烟，

沾衣花气，

恼梦梅魂。

似湘水行春洛神②，

遇天台采药刘晨③。

愁缕成痕，

一枕余香，

半醉黄昏。

---

① 南浦：《楚辞·九歌》："送美人兮南浦。"
② 洛神：洛水之神宓妃，曹植有《洛神赋》赞美她。
③ 刘晨：传说他和阮肇在天台山采药时遇见神仙。

(II) On Celebration Tower

Like fleecy cloud flying down from the southern sky,

Her shadow fair reveals she's shy.

Refraining from smile, she begins to sigh.

Orchid scent around her forehead,

Her dress fragrant with flowers overspread,

The soul of mume blossom disturbs her dream.

She looks like the goddess in love along the stream,

And meets her lover, herb in hand, in fairy land.

A wreath of gloom has left its trace,

The pillow hides her leftover grace.

Half drunk, in twilight she is sunk.

（三）客窗清明

风风雨雨梨花，

窄索帘栊，

巧小窗纱。

甚情绪灯前，

客怀枕畔。

心事天涯！

三千丈清霜鬓发[①]，

五十年春梦繁华[②]。

蓦见人家，

杨柳分烟，

扶上檐牙。

[①] 三千丈清霜鬓发：化用唐代李白《秋浦歌》："白发三千丈，缘愁似个长。"
[②] 春梦繁华：只有在春梦中才出现过繁华的景象。诗人作此曲时，已是民生凋敝，百姓生活惨淡。

(III) Roaming on Mourning Day

Pear blossoms fade in wind and rain.

On narrow window frame I lean

By delicate window screen.

In what mood before lamplight can I remain?

A roamer whose head on the pillow lies,

And whose heart to the end of the earth flies.

My grief as long as an old man's hair white,

Fifty years have passed like a vernal dream overnight.

Suddenly a house comes to sight,

Where smokelike willow leaves

Adorn the tilting eaves.

（四）荆溪即事

问荆溪[①]溪上人家，

为甚人家

不种梅花？

老树支门，

荒蒲绕岸，

苦竹圈笆。

寺无僧狐狸样[②]瓦。

官无事乌鼠当衙[③]。

白水黄沙，

倚遍阑干，

数尽啼鸦。

---

① 荆溪：在今天的江苏省宜兴市南。
② 样：应作"漾"，是抛、弄的意思。
③ 官无事乌鼠当衙：官员不理政事，却让乌鼠之辈兴风作浪。乌鼠：指作恶的小吏差役。

(IV) The Riverside Land

I ask people by the riverside why

Mume trees are not

Planted near by.

The trunk of old mume tree is used to support the door,

Wild weeds are overgrown along the shore.

Dreary is the bamboo-fenced cot.

On the roof of the godless temple foxes trot;

Officials doing nothing let rats run in the hall.

Around the yellow sand white water flows.

Leaning on the balustrade, I count all

The crying crows.

满庭芳

渔父词

乔 吉

（一）

携鱼换酒，

鱼鲜可口，

酒热扶头[①]。

盘中不是鲸鲵肉，

鲟鲊初熟[②]。

太湖水光摇酒瓯[③]。

洞庭山影落鱼舟。

归来后，

一竿钓钩，

不挂古今愁。

---

① 酒热扶头：热酒容易让人喝醉。扶头：使人醉。
② 盘中不是鲸鲵肉，鲟鲊初熟：古代君王讨伐逆贼胜利之后，都要杀鲸或鲵以示警戒。而自己的盘中是寻常的鲟鱼、鲊鱼，自己的生活也与朝中要事无关。
③ 酒瓯：乘酒的器具。

Tune: Courtyard Full of Fragrance

Song of a Fisherman

Qiao Ji

(I)

I bring fish to buy wine:

Fish delicious and fine,

Strong wine intoxicates.

I have no meat of whale in my plates

But sturgeon salted or just fried.

The waves of the lake make my wine cup shake;

The shadows of hills fall by my boatside.

Come back ashore,

I bring my rod with fishing line,

Careless of sorrow now and of yore.

（二）

江声撼①枕，

一川残月，

满目遥岑②。

白云流水无人禁，

胜似山林。

钓晚霞寒波濯锦，

看秋潮夜海镕金。

村醪③窨④，

何人共饮？

鸥鹭是知心。

① 撼：震撼，指江水澎湃。
② 岑：小而高的山。
③ 村醪：自己酿造的浊酒。醪：汁滓混合的酒。
④ 窨：酿好，熟了。

(II)

Waves make my pillow quiver,

The moon wanes on the river,

I see far-off hills shiver.

None could forbid running water or floating cloud;

I'm better than the lord of woods or mountains proud.

The rainbow cloud steeped in cold waves look like brocades;

The autumn moon like molten gold on the sea fades.

Who will drink my home-brew

Together with me?

Who but the gull of the sea.

殿前欢

登江山第一楼

乔 吉

拍阑干,
雾花吹鬓海风寒,
浩歌惊得浮云散。
细数青山,
指蓬莱一望间。
纱巾岸①,
鹤背骑来惯②。
举头长啸,
直上天坛③。

---

① 纱巾岸:纱巾高竿。
② 鹤背骑来惯:惯于骑鹤遨游。
③ 天坛:天空。

Tune: Joy before Palace

The First Tower of the Land

Qiao Ji

I beat on rails,

The foggy wind blows on my hair and the sea wails

I croon aloud, dispersing startled cloud.

Counting the mountains blue,

I point to fairy isles coming in view.

Wearing my silk hood high,

I'm used on the crane's back to fly.

Raising my head, I utter a long sigh,

And straight ascend the sky.

小桃红

效联珠格[①]

乔 吉

落花飞絮隔朱帘,
帘静重门掩。
掩镜羞看脸儿倩,
倩[②]眉尖,
眉尖指屈将归期念。
念他抛闪,
闪咱少欠,
欠你病恹恹。

[①] 联珠格:一种艺术手法,上句的末字和下句首字用字相同,而且连贯至尾。这种手法给人连贯、婉转的感觉。
[②] 倩:美丽的样子。

Tune: Red Peach Blossoms

In Tip-to-toe Style

Qiao Ji

Petals fall with willow down outside the screen,

The screen is still and on closed door I lean.

Leaning beside the mirror, I feel shy,

Shy to see my beautiful face, I sigh.

Sighing, I count when my lord will be,

Will be back to see me.

O me who wonder only,

Only how he can leave me lonely.

水仙子[①]

寻 梅

乔 吉

冬前冬后几村庄,
溪北溪南两履霜,
树头树底孤山[②]上。
冷风来何处香?
忽相逢缟袂绡裳[③]。
酒醒寒惊梦[④],
笛[⑤]凄春断肠,
淡月昏黄。

① 水仙子:曲牌名,又名"凌波仙""凌波曲""湘妃怨"等。
② 孤山:在杭州西湖边。宋人林逋隐居此地,旧时多梅花。
③ 绡裳:薄绸做的裙。
④ 酒醒寒惊梦:传说隋代赵师雄迁居罗浮山下,一个冬天的傍晚,他在醉醒之间遇见一个素服淡妆、语言清丽的女子,并与她共饮。第二天早晨却发现自己睡在一棵大梅树下。
⑤ 笛:指笛曲《梅花落》,汉乐府横吹曲名。

Tune: Song of Daffodils

Seeking for Mume Blossoms

Qiao Ji

From village to village through hoar winter I go;

North and south of the stream my shoes are white with snow.

Where but in Lonely Hill can I find her fair from tip to toe?

Her fragrance comes when I feel the cold wind blow.

Suddenly I meet her in silk robe and white sleeves.

Sober from wine, I wake from dreams, but then she leaves.

My heart is broken to hear the flute wail

In twilight when the moon turns pale.

水仙子

为友人作

乔 吉

搅柔肠离恨病相兼,

重聚首佳期卦怎占?

豫章城①开了座相思店。

闷勾肆②儿逐日添,

愁行货顿塌③在眉尖。

税钱④比⑤茶船上欠,

斤两去等秤上掂。

吃紧的⑥历册般拘钤⑦。

---

① 豫章城:双渐、苏卿相恋故事。传说宋代庐江歌伎苏卿与书生双渐相好,却被茶商冯魁夺去。后来双渐成了县令,再次遇到苏卿,两人才得以相聚。
② 勾肆:勾栏瓦肆,宋代兴起的兼有商业性质的大型综合娱乐场所。
③ 顿塌:囤积居奇。
④ 税钱:比喻相思。
⑤ 比:旧时用来称金银的小秤。
⑥ 吃紧的:的确,实在是。
⑦ 拘钤:钳制,管制。

Tune: Song of Daffodils

Written for a Friend

Qiao Ji

Illness and parting grief disturb your tender heart.

When can you meet again now you are kept apart?

You may open a lovesick shop in southern town,

And go to seek amusement when grief weighs you down.

But grief like goods is stored up on your eyebrow.

How can you pay the tax on the tea?

How can you slide the weight on the steel yard?

To change account books is really hard.

雁儿落过得胜令

忆 别

乔 吉

（一）雁儿落

殷勤红叶诗①，
冷淡黄花市。
清江天水笺②，
白雁云烟字③。

---

① 红叶诗：唐宪宗时有宫人在红叶上题诗："殷勤寄红叶，好去到人间。"红叶从水沟里流出，为人所拾，二人最后成为夫妻。
② 天水笺：天和水茫茫一片，好像一幅巨大的信笺。
③ 白雁云烟字：天空中一行行白雁，就像云烟写在天上的字。

From "Falling Swan" to "Triumphant Song"

Farewell Recalled

Qiao Ji

(I) Tune: Falling Swan

Thank you for your verse on leaf red
In cold place where yellow blooms spread.
Clear stream and sky are paper white,
On which wild geese and clouds write.

（二）得胜令

游子去何之？
无处寄新词。
酒醒灯昏夜，
窗寒梦觉时。
寻思①，
谈笑十年事；
嗟咨②，
风流两鬓丝。

① 寻思：怀想，思念。
② 嗟咨：感叹。

(II) Tune: Triumphant Song

Where have you gone since our adieu?

Where can I send you my verse new?

Sober from wine when lamplight gleams,

By window cold I wake from dreams.

I pass

In mind what happened these ten years.

Alas!

On my forehead grey hair appears.

集贤宾

乔 吉

(一) 咏柳忆别

恨青青画桥东畔柳,
曾祖送①少年游。
散晴雪杨花清昼,
又一场心事悠悠。
翠丝长不系雕鞍,
碧云寒空掩珠楼。
揎②罗袖试将纤玉手,
绾③东风摇损轻柔。
同心方胜④结,
缨络绣文球⑤。

① 祖送:饯行,送别。祖:指古人出行前祭祀的路神。
② 揎:卷起。
③ 绾:同"挽",系住。
④ 同心方胜:以两块斜方形彩绸折成的心形饰物。
⑤ 缨络绣文球:古代妇女的头饰,是用线结成的,下面坠有绣着花纹的布球。

Tune: Meeting of Good Friends

Qiao Ji

(I) Parting under Willows Recalled

East of the bridge we do not like the willows green.
How many parting lovers they have seen!
Willow down wafts like snow on sunny day,
My heart is gone with it far, far away.
The willow twigs, though long, cannot retain
His parting steed; green clouds veil the bower in vain.
I roll up my sleeves and pluck with my hands fair
A tender sprig swaying in the east wind, where
I see two hearts into a knot are tied
And an embroidered ball hangs by the side.

（二）逍遥乐

绾不成鸳鸯双扣，

空惊散梢头

一双锦鸠。

何处忘忧？

听枝上数声黄栗留[①]，

怕不[②]弄春娇巧啭歌喉？

惊回好梦，

题起离情，

唤醒闲愁。

[①] 黄栗留：黄鹂。
[②] 怕不：岂不是。

(II) Tune: Joy of Freedom

Now I cannot tie a lovebirds' knot,

But startle a pair of birds in love

On the tip of the tree above.

How can my grief be forgot?

I listen to golden orioles sing,

They remind me of the sweet songs of spring.

But I'm afraid they would break

Your dream and wake

Your parting grief on the green leaf.

（三）醋葫芦

雨晴珠泪收，
烟颦翠黛羞①。
殢②风流还自怨风流。
病多不奈秋，
未秋来早先消瘦。
晓风残月在帘钩。

① 烟颦翠黛羞：女子皱眉的样子。颦：皱眉。翠黛：女子的眉毛。
② 殢：留恋。

(III) Tune: A Gourd of Vinegar

My tears are dried after the rain,
My frowning eyebrows shy remain,
Loving and complaining of the flowing breeze.
Ill in autumn, how can I feel at ease?
Before autumn comes, how languid I look!
Like the waning moon hanging on the hook.

（四）浪里来煞

不要你护雕阑花甃①香,
荫苍苔石径幽,
只要你盼行人
终日替我凝眸,
只要你重温灞陵②别后酒。
如今时候,
只要向绿阴深处缆归舟。

① 花甃：雕花的井壁。
② 灞陵：在长安东郊的灞水边上，人们送别常常送到灞桥，折柳赠别。

(IV) Epilogue: Coming with Waves

I don't want you to lean on fragrant balustrade,
Or stand on mossy, stony path in the green shade.
I want you to gaze afar and wait all day long,
To remember our farewell feast and farewell song.
As for today,
I want you to tie your boat in the green shade,
When you return from far away.

殿前欢

刘时中

醉颜酡^①,

太翁庄上走如梭。

门前几个官人坐,

有虎皮驮驮^②。

呼王留唤伴哥^③,

无一个,空叫得喉咙破。

人踏了瓜果,马践了田禾。

---

① 醉颜酡:喝醉了脸红彤彤的样子。酡:红色。
② 虎皮驮驮:指游牧民族使用的虎皮包。驮驮:沉重的样子。
③ 王留、伴哥:元人对农村青年的泛称。

Tune: Joy before Palace

Liu Shizhong

With face drunk red,
In village elder's house tax-collectors come and go.
Some officials sit in the hall,
With heavy bags of tiger skin piled up below.
They call the roll, but none answers at all.
They shout and cry
Until their throats go dry.
Then soldiers would damage the crop and horses tread
The field so that nothing could grow.

落梅风

阿鲁威

千年志,
一旦空。
唯有纸钱灰晚风吹送。
尽①蜀鹃血啼烟树中,
唤不回一场春梦②。

① 尽:任凭。
② 春梦:比喻繁华似锦的人生。

Tune: Wind of Falling Mume Blossoms

A Luwei

A thousand years later,

All will pass in laughter.

Only burnt paper money would waft in the breeze.

Though cuckoos cry out blood among the mist-veiled trees,

How could they retain

A vernal dream vain?

醉太平

寒 食

王元鼎

声声啼乳鸦,
生叫破韶华。
夜深微雨润堤沙,
香风万家。
画楼洗尽鸳鸯瓦,
彩绳半湿秋千架。
觉来红日上窗纱,
听街头卖杏花。

① 醉太平：曲调名，又名"凌波曲"。
② 韶华：春光。
③ 鸳鸯瓦：屋顶上的瓦一俯一仰互相搭扣，故称"鸳鸯瓦"。

Tune: Drunk in Time of Peace

Cold Food Day

Wang Yuanding

Nursling crows caw out cry on cry,

Breaking the early day of spring.

Last night the drizzle moistened the sand far and nigh,

Thousands of homes sweetened by the breeze on the wing.

The lovebirds tiles of painted house are washed clean,

The colored ropes of the swing wet before the bower.

I wake to find the sun redden the window screen

And hear the street cry of selling apricot flower.

塞鸿秋

薛昂夫

功名万里忙如燕,
斯文一脉^①微如线。
光阴寸隙流如电,
风霜两鬓白如练。
尽道便休官,
林下何曾见^②?
至今寂寞彭泽县^③。

---

① 斯文:本指周朝的礼乐制度,后指礼让文雅,品格高尚。一脉:一支。
② 尽道便休官,林下何曾见:大家都说要辞官归隐,但是隐居的山林中哪里有他们。
③ 彭泽县:指陶渊明,他曾任彭泽县令,后辞官隐居。

Tune: Autumn Swan on Frontier

Xue Angfu

Busy for far-flung fame as swallows in flight,

Culture hangs by a thread, none cares to be polite.

Time flies away as fast as flashing light,

Like frosted silk the hair on our forehead turns white.

All say it is good to retire,

But to be a hermit none has the desire.

Up to now only

The poet-hermit still feels lonely.

楚天遥过清江引 [1]

送 春

薛昂夫

（一）楚天遥

有意送春归，
无计留春住[2]。
明年又着来，
何似休归去？
桃花也解愁，
点点飘红玉[3]。
目断楚天[4]遥，
不见春归路。

---

[1] 楚天遥过清江引：为双调，由《楚天遥》和《清江引》两支曲子组成。
[2] 无计留春住：宋代欧阳修有《蝶恋花》："雨横风狂三月暮，门掩黄昏，无计留春住。"
[3] 红玉：飘落的桃花。
[4] 楚天：南方的天空。

From "Far-flung Southern Sky" to "Song of Clear River"

Farewell to Spring

Xue Angfu

(I) Tune: Far-flung Southern Sky

I have a mind to say farewell to spring,

But I have no means to stay her lingering.

Spring will come back again next year,

Would it not be better to stay forever here?

Peach blossoms seem to know my grief,

Falling like red jade petal on petal, leaf on leaf.

I gaze as far as the Southern sky,

But I can't see the way spring will go by.

（二）清江引

春若有情春更苦[①]，

暗里韶光度。

夕阳山外山，

春水渡傍渡[②]。

不知那答儿是春住处[③]。

[①] 春若有情春更苦：套用唐代李贺《金铜仙人辞汉歌》"天若有情天亦老"句。
[②] 夕阳山外山，春水渡傍渡：用宋代戴复古《世事》"春水渡傍渡，夕阳山外山"句。傍：通"旁"。
[③] 不知那答儿是春住处：活用宋代黄庭坚《清平乐·晚春》："若有人知春去处，换取归来同住。"

(II) Tune: Song of Clear River

If spring had a heart, she would feel sadder still

To see time fly away,

The sun go down from hill to hill,

And water flow from rill to rill.

But where, where is the place for her to stay?

金字经

吴弘道

（一）

落花风飞去，
故枝①依旧鲜。
月缺终须有再圆。
圆，
月圆人未圆。
朱颜变，
几时得重少年?

① 故枝：旧枝，指花落后的树枝。

Tune: Golden Canon

Wu Hongdao

(I)

Fallen petals fly away with the breeze,

But leaves are still fresh on the trees.

The waning moon will wax again,

Wax and wane,

But we can't gather round as the moon waxes round.

Rosy faces to grow old are bound,

But where could youth be refound?

（二）

这家春醪尽，
那家醅瓮①开。
卖了肩头一担柴。
咳！
酒钱怀里揣。
葫芦在，
大家提去来。

① 醅瓮：酒坛子。

(II)

No more village brew?

Undistilled wine will do.

The wood I cut sold out,

Heigh!

I'll have money in my pocket, no doubt.

If you want to drink, you need not pay,

But take your gourd and follow my way.

拨不断

闲 乐

吴弘道

（一）

泛浮槎①，寄生涯，

长江万里秋风驾。

稚子和烟②煮嫩茶，

老妻带月炰③新鲊④，

醉时闲话。

（二）

利名无，

宦情疏，

彭泽升斗微官禄。

蠹鱼⑤食残架上书。

晓霜荒尽篱边菊，

罢官归去。

① 泛浮槎：放舟漫游。浮槎：木筏，小船。
② 和烟：置身炊烟之中。和：掺杂。
③ 炰：蒸煮。
④ 鲊：腌渍的鱼。
⑤ 蠹鱼：蛀蚀书籍衣服的一种小虫，银白色有点像鱼，故名。

Tune: Unbroken String

Leisure and Pleasure

Wu Hongdao

(I)

I pass my life
On floating raft
Steered by the autumn breeze on the river with pleasure.
Despite the smoke, my young son is brewing tea aft;
Cooking fish in moonlight, busy is my wife.
Drunk, we talk at leisure.

(II)

Careless of gain and fame,
To rank I lay no claim.
Poet Tao would not in official work be lost,
Nor let bookworms eat holes in his books,
Nor his chrysanthemums be bitten by frost,
He returned to his nooks.

沉醉东风
秋日湘阴①道中

赵善庆

山对面兰堆翠岫,
草齐腰绿染沙洲。
傲霜橘柚青,
濯雨②兼葭秀。
隔沧波隐隐红楼。
点破潇湘万顷秋,
是几叶儿传黄败柳③。

① 湘阴:今湖南岳阳市湘阴县。
② 濯雨:被雨洗。
③ 传黄败柳:泛黄的柳叶。

Tune: Intoxicated in East Wind

An Autumn Day on My Way to Xiangyin

Zhao Shanqing

In face I see green hills piled up on hills green,
Nearby grass grows waist-deep and grassy isles are seen.
Frost-proof tangerines and shaddocks stand proud,
Reeds steeped in rain look clear and clean.
Across the waves the riverside tower dimmed by cloud,
Peeping through boundless autumn on the river, it grieves
To see a few withered willow leaves.

折桂令

湖山堂[①]

赵善庆

八窗开水月交光,

诗酒坛台,

莺燕排场。

歌扇摇风,

梨云飘雪[②],

粉黛生香。

红烛台已更旧邦,

白头民犹说新堂。

花妒幽芳,

人换宫妆[③]。

唯有湖山,

不管兴亡。

[①] 湖山堂:应在杭州西湖。
[②] 梨云飘雪:字面意思是,梨花飘落时,纷纷洁白如雪。这里用来渲染歌舞纷繁。
[③] 换宫妆:指歌女们的打扮变成了正流行的宫妆,暗指社会动荡,朝代更迭。

Tune: Plucking Laurel Branch

Hall of Lake and Hill

Zhao Shanqing

Outside eight windows water dissolves in moonlight,

Orioles and swallows dance on the stage in a line

Before poets and drinkers of wine.

The dancers' fans bring a breeze light,

They dance like clouds or pear blossoms white,

With fragrance sweet their powdered faces spread.

The old state replaced by the new with candles red,

The white-haired still remember its newly built hall.

Dancers in their changed palace attire

Awaken envious flowers' desire,

But lakes and hills care not for the state's rise and fall.

庆东原

泊罗阳驿

赵善庆

砧声①住,
蛩韵切,
静寥寥门掩清秋夜。
秋心凤阙②,
秋愁雁堞③,
秋梦蝴蝶。
十载故乡心,
一夜邮亭月。

① 砧声:古代妇女为备置冬衣捣练的声音。
② 凤阙:指京城。本句暗指诗人此时仍然心系国事。
③ 雁堞:谓城墙如同雁阵一样排列着。堞:城头上齿状的矮墙。

Tune: Blessed East Plain

Moored by the Post

Zhao Shanqing

The beetles still,

The crickets trill,

Clear autumn shut outdoors in night tranquil.

Where is the Phoenix Tower high?

Grieved to see parapet nigh,

I dream to be a butterfly.

My homesickness for ten long years

In tonight's alien dream appears.

柳营曲

太平即事

马谦斋

亲凤塔,

住龙沙^①,

天下太平无事也。

辞却公衙,

别了京华,

甘分老农家。

傲河阳潘岳栽花,

效东门邵平^②种瓜。

庄前栽果木,

山下种桑麻。

度岁华,

活计老生涯。

---

① 亲凤塔,住龙沙：指天下太平,边塞安定。凤塔：本指宫内楼阁,后指代宫阙。
   龙沙：本指西北边远山地和沙漠地区,这里指边塞疆场。
② 邵平：秦代东陵侯,秦灭亡后沦为布衣,就在长安城东种瓜自给。

Tune: Song of Willow Camp

Written in Time of Peace

Ma Qianzhai

By Phoenix Tower's side,

With frontiers pacified,

What with the world in peace can I do after all?

My office resigned,

Leaving the capital,

I'm glad again a rural life to find.

Too proud to imitate the poet planting flowers,

I will grow melon outside the east door.

With fruit-bearing trees before my bowers,

And mulberries at the foot of the hill,

I will pass still

The rest of my years as of yore.

人月圆

山中书事

张可久

兴亡千古繁华梦,

诗眼①倦天涯。

孔林乔木,

吴宫蔓草,

楚庙寒鸦②。

数间茅舍,

藏书万卷,

投老③村家。

山中何事?

松花酿酒,

春水煎茶。

---

① 诗眼:诗人独具观察力的眼光。
② 孔林乔木,吴宫蔓草,楚庙寒鸦:指昔日的繁华已成过眼云烟,只剩下草木寒鸦。孔林:山东曲阜孔子墓地。吴宫:三国时期吴国的宫殿。楚庙:战国时期楚国的宗庙。
③ 投老:到老的时候。

Tune: Man and Moon

Written in the Mountain

Zhang Kejiu

The rise and fall from year to year are but vain dreams.

A poet's eyes are tired of roaming on the streams.

The sage's forest grows old,

The ancient palace overrun with weed,

The temple crows feel cold.

A few rooms in a cot are what I need;

With my ten thousand books,

I'll retire in my nooks.

What can I do in the mountain?

With leaves of pine

I'll brew my wine,

And make my tea with vernal water from the fountain.

人月圆

春晚次韵

张可久

萋萋①芳草春云乱,

愁在夕阳中。

短亭别酒,

平湖画舫,

垂柳骄骢②。

一声啼鸟,

一番夜雨,

一阵东风。

桃花吹尽,

佳人何在?

门掩残红。

① 萋萋:草茂盛的样子。
② 骢:青白色的骏马。

Tune: Man and Moon

Rhyming with Friend in Late Spring

Zhang Kejiu

Lush, lush sweet grass and spring clouds spread pellmell;

Grief seems exhaled by setting sunlight.

In the pavilion where we drank farewell,

I see no painted boat on the calm lake afloat,

Nor the proud steed neighing beneath willow trees.

I only hear the cry of birds in fright,

The dripping rain leftover last night,

And the sigh of the eastern breeze.

All the peach flowers are blown away.

Where is the beauty of the bygone day?

Within the closed door only the fallen reds stay.

人月圆

春日湖上

张可久

小楼还被青山碍①,
隔断楚天遥。
昨宵入梦,
那人如玉,
何处吹箫?
门前朝暮,
无情秋月,
有信春潮。
看看憔悴,
飞花心事,
残柳眉梢。

---

① 小楼还被青山碍:从小楼上远望,不料被层叠的青山阻挡了视线。

Tune: Man and Moon

A Spring Day on the Lake

Zhang Kejiu

From my bower girt with mountains green,

The far-off Southern sky cannot be seen.

My love as fair as jade white

Came into my dream last night.

Where is she now playing on the flute far away?

Before the door night and day,

I see but heartless autumn moon

And faithful vernal tide at noon.

How languid now am I!

My heart like flowers that can't fly,

My eyebrows like willow leaves dry.

醉太平

怀 古

张可久

翩翩野舟,

泛泛沙鸥。

登临不尽古今愁,

白云去留。

凤凰台上青山旧①,

秋千墙里垂杨瘦②,

琵琶亭畔野花秋③。

长江自流。

---

① 凤凰台上青山旧:失意怀古的诗仙已经逝去了,只有青山还像当年一样屹立在远处。李白天宝年间被放逐后,游历金陵,写下了《登金陵凤凰台》:"凤凰台上凤凰游,凤去台空江自流",抒发自己的失意心情。
② 秋千墙里垂杨瘦:苏轼在元丰年间,在被贬的途中写过《蝶恋花》:"墙里秋千墙外道,墙外行人,墙里佳人笑。"以佳人无情,比喻自己有报国心却不被重用。
③ 琵琶亭畔野花秋:用白居易作《琵琶行》一诗的典故。

Tune: Drunk in Time of Peace

Thinking of the Past

Zhang Kejiu

A floating boat,
A gull carefree,
I climb the height with endless sorrow old and new,
White clouds linger with me.
From Phoenix Tower I find the changeless hills blue;
Beside the swing within the wall
The weeping willow slender grows;
Before the pavilion late autumn flowers fall,
But heedless, the endless river still flows.

醉太平

感 怀

张可久

人皆嫌①命窘,
谁不见钱亲?
水晶环入面糊盆②,
才沾粘便滚。
文章糊了盛钱囤③,
门庭改作迷魂阵,
清廉贬入睡馄饨,
葫芦提倒稳④。

① 嫌:厌恶嫌弃。
② 水晶环入面糊盆:一个个水晶环掉进面糊盆,不能滚动。比喻一个个聪明人陷进钱眼里,无法自拔。
③ 文章糊了盛钱囤:比喻将读书做文章当作是赚钱的工具。
④ 葫芦提倒稳:糊里糊涂,不会费心算计赚钱的日子倒是最稳当。

Tune: Drunk in Time of Peace

Reflection

Zhang Kejiu

Poverty is disliked by all.
Is money not dear to you?
If a crystal ring in a pot of paste should fall,
Could it not be pasted in view?
If a writer advertises for a millionaire,
His soul is puzzled with money and renown.
A sleepy head cannot be fair and square,
It would be safer to hold a gourd upside down.

锦橙梅

张可久

红馥馥①的脸衬霞,
黑髭髭的鬓堆鸦②。
料应他,
必是个中人③,
打扮的堪④描画。
颤巍巍的插着翠花,
宽绰绰的穿着轻纱。
兀的不风韵煞人也啊!
是谁家?
我不住了偷睛儿抹。

① 红馥馥:红艳艳,而且香气浓烈,比喻美人如花朵一般明艳馥郁。
② 堆鸦:凸起的发髻浓密乌黑,如同乌鸦的羽毛乌黑闪亮。
③ 个中人:指歌姬舞女。
④ 堪:值得。

Tune: Orange and Mume on Brocade

Zhang Kejiu

Her perfumed pink cheeks look like rosy cloud,

Her ebony chignon like black crows in crowd.

I guess

She must be a songstress

In such a picturesque attire.

Her emerald headdress quivers with each pace,

Her dainty silken robe is large and light.

How bewitching is she walking in delight!

How could I not steal glances at her face?

How could I quench my insatiable desire?

迎仙客
秋 夜
张可久

雨乍晴,
月笼明,
秋香院落砧杵鸣①。
二三更,
千万声,
捣碎离情,
不管愁人听。

---

① 砧杵鸣:捣衣的声音,砧杵捣练是古代妇女的日常劳动,秋季捣练是为在外的征人赶制寒衣,因而具有特殊的意义。

Tune: Greeting a Fairy Guest

Autumn Night

Zhang Kejiu

After rain it turns fine,

All steeped in bright moonshine.

The fragrant autumn courtyard hears the beetles pound.

Deeper, deeper the night,

Deeper, deeper the sound.

It breaks the heart of those who part,

But cares not for their plight.

红绣鞋

宁元帅席上

张可久

鸣玉珮凌烟图画①,

乐云林投老②生涯。

少年谁识故侯家?

青蛇昏③宝剑,

团锦碎④袍花,

飞龙闲⑤厩马。

---

① 鸣玉珮凌烟图画:年轻时希望自己青云直上,跻身高官王侯之列。凌烟:指凌烟阁,是唐太宗悬挂开国元勋画像的表彰他们的地方。
② 投老:临老。
③ 昏:昏暗无光。
④ 碎:杂乱,零碎。
⑤ 闲:栏杆,这里指约束。

Tune: Embroidered Red Shoes

At the Feast of Marshal Ning

Zhang Kejiu

I longed to ring my pendants in the Gallery.
Now old, the forest under white cloud pleases me.
Who of the youth still knows the ancient heroes' deeds?
Their precious swords like blue serpents fade,
Broken to pieces are their robes of brocade,
The flying dragons now become stabled steeds.

红绣鞋

虎丘①道上

张可久

船系谁家古岸,
人归何处青山。
且将诗做图画看:
雁声芦叶老,
鹭影蓼花寒,
鹤巢松树晚。

---

① 虎丘:在江苏苏州西北,传说吴王阖闾葬在那里。

Tune: Embroidered Red Shoes

On My Way to the Tiger Hill

Zhang Kejiu

Where may I moor my boat along the ancient shore?

Where is my friend in the blue mountains I adore?

Can I draw pictures in poetic lines?

At the song of wild geese the reed grows old,

At the sight of herons the knotweed feels cold,

At dusk the cranes return to their nest amid the pines.

梧叶儿

湖山夜景

张可久

猿啸黄昏后,
人行画卷中。
萧寺罢①疏钟,
湿翠横千峰。
清风响万松,
寒玉奏孤桐。
身在秋香月宫。

① 罢:停息,没有。

Tune: Plane Leaves

Lake and Hills at Night

Zhang Kejiu

After dusk apes sing,

Men seem to go along a screen,

No temple bells ring.

Peaks on peaks like bars in wet green,

Pines echo with the breeze,

Cold jade plays on lonely plane trees.

I seem to be in the Moon Palace Hall

Turning fragrant in the fall.

梧叶儿

有所思

张可久

人何处?
草自香,
弦索已生尘。
柳线萦离思,
荷衣①拭泪痕。
梅屋锁吟魂。
目断吴山暮云。

① 荷衣:绿色的衣服。

Tune: Plane Leaves

Thinking of the Lutist

Zhang Kejiu

Where is my lutist bright?

Grass grows again in spring,

But dust covers the lute's string,

The parting grief embodied in willow leaves,

She wipes her tears away with lotus sleeves.

My soul can only croon in the mume bower white,

The cloud-veiled Southern mountains lost to sight.

折桂令

西陵①送别

张可久

画船儿载不起离愁,

人到西陵,

恨满东州。

懒上归鞍,

慵开泪眼,

怕倚层楼。

春去春来,

管送别依依岸柳;

潮生潮落,

会忘机②泛泛沙鸥。

烟水悠悠,

有句相酬,

无计相留。

---

① 西陵:应是浙江萧山之西的西兴镇,古称西陵。
② 机:心机,坏心眼。

Tune: Plucking Laurel Branch

Farewell at the West Ferry

Zhang Kejiu

Our parting grief outweighs your painted boat.
I'm still at Ferry West,
Your sorrow eastward flows.
On my steed I won't ride,
Nor open tearful eyes.
I fear to lean on rails of tower high.
Spring comes and goes,
The willow trees by riverside
Are grieved to say goodbye.
The tide may fall and rise,
The heartless gulls still float.
The mist-veiled water runs without rest.
I can write verse for you,
But how could we not say adieu?

折桂令

九 日[①]

张可久

对青山强整乌纱[②],

归雁横秋,

倦客思家。

翠袖殷勤[③],

金杯错落,

玉手琵琶。

人老去西风白发,

蝶愁来明日黄花。

回首天涯,

一抹斜阳,

数点寒鸦。

---

① 九日：农历九月九日的重阳节，是登高团聚的日子。
② 乌纱：乌纱帽，初为官帽，后流行民间，不分贵贱都可以佩戴。
③ 翠袖殷勤：宋代晏几道《鹧鸪天》："彩袖殷勤捧玉钟。"

Tune: Plucking Laurel Branch

The Mountain-climbing Day

Zhang Kejiu

Before blue hills I put down my official hat;

Returning wild geese fly across the autumn sky.

How can a tired roamer not think of his own flat?

Though the rainbow-colored sleeves try

To fill my golden cup with wine,

And jade-like hands play on lute fine,

I'm growing old, my white hair wafts when west wind blows.

Tomorrow yellow blooms will sadden butterflies.

Looking back to the far-flung skies,

I find the setting sun in bloody dye,

Dotted with a few chilly crows.

折桂令

次 韵

张可久

唤西施伴我西游,
客路依依,
烟水悠悠。
翠树啼鹃,
青天旅雁,
白雪盟鸥①。
人倚梨花病酒,
月明杨柳维舟。
试上层楼,
绿满江南,
红褪春愁。

① 盟鸥:与鸥鸟为盟友,比喻隐退。

Tune: Plucking Laurel Branch

Rhyming with a Friend

Zhang Kejiu

I'd call the Beauty to go to the west with me.
How can I not delay on the winding long way
Along the careless mist-veiled stream, carefree?
The cuckoos cry amid green trees,
The blue sky streaked by wild geese,
The gulls are friendly with snow white.
Drunk, I lean on pear trees in blossoms bright,
But willow trigs cannot tie the boat with moonlight.
I try to go upstairs to gaze far, far away,
But find the Southern Rivershore with green overspread
And vernal grief fading in fallen red.

折桂令

村庵①即事

张可久

掩柴门啸傲烟霞②,
隐隐林峦,
小小仙家,
楼外白云,
窗前翠竹,
井底朱砂③。
五亩宅无人种瓜,
一村庵有客分茶。
春色无多,
开到蔷薇,
落尽梨花。

---

① 村庵：村中的小屋。古代文人读书的地方也叫庵。
② 烟霞：云烟彩霞。
③ 井底朱砂：指隐士学道炼丹的生活场景。朱砂：道家炼丹需要用朱砂为原料。井：丹井，用来装药炼丹的井状容器。

Tune: Plucking Laurel Branch

Rural Life

Zhang Kejiu

Wicker gate closed, I'm proud to

Croon 'neath rainbow cloud.

Forest and peaks dimly appear,

With fairy cottages far and near.

White clouds beyond my bower overspread;

Before my window green bamboos stand,

In the tripod is left cinnabar red.

None of my household grows melon in the waste land,

In my cot I drink tea with my friends day by day.

Spring has nearly passed away.

After the blooming rose, now all

The pear blossoms will fall.

水仙子

梅边即事

张可久

好花多向雨中开,
佳客新从云外①来。
清诗未了年前债,
相逢且放怀。
曲栏杆碾②玉亭白,
小树粉蝶翅,
苍苔点绿胎,
踏碎青鞋。

① 云外:比喻很远的地方。
② 碾:紧紧地环绕。

Tune: Song of Daffodils

Drinking by Mume Trees

Zhang Kejiu

Good flowers will open in the rain;

Good friends from afar come again.

In rhyming with your verse I owe you a year-old debt.

Let us drink our fill now we've met.

The balustrade winds round the bower of carved jade,

Over young trees butterflies flit about.

The ground dotted with green moss looks like deer skin.

Let us tread on it till our shoes are worn out.

小桃红

离 情

张可久

几场秋雨老①黄花,
不管离人怕②。
一曲哀弦泪双下,
放琵琶。
挑灯羞看围屏画,
声悲玉马,
愁新罗帕,
恨不到天涯③。

① 老：使得……老。
② 怕：忧愁。
③ 恨不到天涯：我恨不得追随你到天涯海角。

Tune: Red Peach Blossoms

Parting Grief

Zhang Kejiu

The autumn rains have oldened yellow flowers,

Careless of those in lonely bowers.

My tears stream down to hear the song played by sad strings,

Putting down the lute and turning on lamplight, I feel shy

To see the picture on the screen

And hear the bell of jade rings.

My grief has wetted the silk handkerchief green.

Why could I not go with you to the end of the sky?

普天乐

西湖即事

张可久

蕊珠宫,
蓬莱洞①。
青松影里,
红藕香中。
千机云锦重,
一片银河冻②。
缥缈佳人双飞凤,
紫箫寒月满长空③。
阑干晚风,
菱歌④上下,
渔火西东。

---

① 蕊珠宫,蓬莱洞:形容西湖景色像仙境一样美丽。蕊珠宫,道教传说中的天宫。蓬莱,传说中的海上仙山。
② 千机云锦重,一片银河冻:形容彩霞映在湖面上,就像织女织出的千重云锦,映在清寒的银河上。
③ 缥缈佳人双飞凤,紫箫寒月满长空:湖上的箫声美妙,仿佛是一对骑着飞凤的仙女在这片月色明亮的夜空中吹奏的。
④ 菱歌:采菱人唱的歌。

Tune: Universal Joy

The West Lake

Zhang Kejiu

The pearly palace hall

In fairy island looms.

In the shade of the green pines tall

Wafts the fragrance of pink lotus blooms.

Cloud on cloud woven in brocade

Like frozen Silver River in the boundless sky,

Two beauties in flowing robes on phoenix wings fly,

And play on violet flute a tune to chill the moon.

The evening breeze caresses the balustrade,

Lotus girls' songs waft low and high,

Fishermen's lanterns float east and west, far and nigh.

普天乐

秋 怀

张可久

会真诗,
相思债。
花笺象管①,
钿盒金钗。
雁啼明月中,
人在青山外。
独上危楼②愁无奈,
起西风一片离怀。
白衣③未来,
东篱好在,
黄菊先开④。

---

① 象管:象牙色的毛笔。
② 危楼:高楼。
③ 白衣:指白衣飘飘的友人。
④ 东篱、黄菊:有晋代陶渊明《饮酒》中"采菊东篱下"的意境。

Tune: Universal Joy

Autumn Thoughts

Zhang Kejiu

Love poems show anew

The debt I owe you.

On flowery paper with ivory pen I write,

With golden hairpin and jewel case in sight.

Wild geese cry past the full moon bright,

But you are beyond the mountains blue.

What with my parting grief can I do?

Up the tower I go.

The west wind cannot blow my grief away.

Will the white-gowned messenger come today?

I have at least the hedge in the east

Where yellow chrysanthems will blow.

喜春来

金华客舍

张可久

落红小雨苍苔径,
飞絮东风细柳营^①,
可怜客里过清明。
不待听,
昨夜杜鹃声。

---

① 细柳营:原指汉文帝大将周亚夫镇守细柳的军营,这里取其春风杨柳的景色,与"苍苔径"相对。

Tune: Welcome to Spring

At an Inn in Jinhua

Zhang Kejiu

A fine rain brings down red flowers on mossy way,

And the west wind blows willow down away.

How sad and drear to pass a lonely Mourning Day!

How could I bear to hear all the night long

The cuckoos' home-going song!

喜春来
永康驿中

张可久

荷盘①敲雨珠千颗,
山背披云玉一梭。
半篇诗景费吟哦,
芳草坡,
松外采茶歌。

① 荷盘:盘子一般的荷叶。

Tune: Welcome to Spring

At an Inn in Yongkang

Zhang Kejiu

Rain beats on lotus leaves drop on drop

Like thousands of pearls without stop.

The mountain's clad in cloud like a cloak of jade.

I try hard to write a verse to describe the scene.

On the slope with grass green,

I hear beyond the pines songs of tea-picking maid.

朝天子

闺 情[①]

张可久

与谁画眉?
猜破风流谜。
铜驼巷里玉骢嘶,
夜半归来醉。
小意[②]收拾,
怪胆[③]矜持,
不识羞谁似你!
自知理亏,
灯下和衣睡。

① 闺情:写少妇明知爱人有了新欢,聪明的她却仍旧贤惠体贴,让爱人自觉惭愧。
② 小意:小心仔细地。
③ 怪胆:故意摆出。

Tune: Skyward Song

A Wife Waiting on Her Lord

Zhang Kejiu

Of whom will you pencil the brow?

I know with whom you are in love now.

Deep in the lane I hear your horse neigh,

Drunk at midnight, you're on your homeward way.

I take great care to make your bed,

But you pretend to turn away your haughty head.

Who is so unashamed as you?

Unworthy, you know it's true

I've done my best,

So by lamplight you lie down, not yet undressed.

山坡羊

闺思

张可久

云松螺髻①,
香温鸳被,
掩春闺一觉伤春睡。
柳花飞,
小琼姬②,
一声"雪下呈祥瑞③"。
团圆梦儿生唤起④。
"谁,
不做美?
呸,
却是你!"

---

① 云松螺髻:指头发松散。云,形容女子浓密柔软的头发。螺髻:梳成螺旋形的发髻。
② 小琼姬:美丽的小丫鬟。
③ 雪下呈祥瑞:瑞雪兆丰年的意思。
④ 生唤起:硬被吵醒。

Tune: Sheep on the Slope

A Wife Bored

Zhang Kejiu

Her chignon loose as cloud,

Her lovebirds quilt with fragrance overflowed,

Her boudoir closed, she's deep in vernal sleep.

Willow down flies,

Her young maid cries:

"Lo! What auspicious snow!"

It wakes her from the dream of her love she will keep.

"Who?

What a bore!

Oh,

It is you."

殿前欢

离 思

张可久

月笼沙,

十年心事付琵琶。

相思懒看帏屏画,

人在天涯。

春残豆蔻花①,

情寄鸳鸯帕②,

香冷荼蘼架③。

旧游台榭,

晓梦窗纱。

---

① 豆蔻花:一种初夏开花的草本植物。曲中以豆蔻比喻未出嫁的少女。
② 情寄鸳鸯帕:将情思寄托在绣着鸳鸯的巾帕上。
③ 香冷荼蘼架:荼蘼夏日开花,但那时已是百花凋零,荼蘼虽然香气袭人,却难免寂寞。本句暗喻青春流逝。

Tune: Joy before Palace

Longing

Zhang Kejiu

The sandbar veiled in moonbeams,

I confide to my lute my tears of ten long years.

Lovesick, I will not gaze on the picturesque screen.

For far away, my love cannot be seen.

Spring wanes with cardamom flower;

I send him a lovebirds handkerchief from my bower.

Now fragrance of raspberry is cold.

Where are the scenic spots of old?

I find but window-screened morning dreams.

清江引

秋 怀

张可久

西风信来家万里[①],
问我归期未。
雁啼红叶天,
人醉黄花地,
芭蕉雨声秋梦里。

① 西风信来家万里:西风从遥远的家乡给我捎来一封家信。

Tune: Song of Clear River

Homesickness in Autumn

Zhang Kejiu

From far-off home a letter comes in western breeze,

Asking me when I can be home-bound.

In the sky reddened by maple leaves cry wild geese,

Drunk amid yellow flowers strewn on the ground,

I hear in autumn dream rain beat banana trees.

天净沙

鲁卿①庵中

张可久

青苔古木萧萧②,
苍云秋水迢迢③,
红叶山斋小小。
有谁曾到?
探梅人④过溪桥。

① 鲁卿:诗人隐居山中的友人。
② 萧萧:冷清幽静的样子。
③ 迢迢:高远的样子。
④ 探梅人:诗人自己。梅,比喻高士,这里暗指自己的友人。

Tune: Sunny Sand

Calling on a Hermit

Zhang Kejiu

Green moss and old trees in deep gloom,

Pale clouds and far-off water loom,

Red leaves cast shade on little room.

Who'd cross the creek but those who seek

The mume in bloom?

一枝花

湖上归

张可久

（一）

长天落彩霞,

远水涵①秋镜。

花如人面红,

山似佛头青②。

生色围屏③,

翠冷④松云径,

嫣然眉黛⑤横。

但携将旖旎浓香⑥,

何必赋横斜瘦影⑦?

① 涵：包涵，包容。
② 佛头青：深青色。佛家传说，佛陀的头发是青色的，称"青螺髻"。
③ 围屏：画屏，屏风。
④ 翠冷：苍翠清冷。
⑤ 眉黛：青色的远山。
⑥ 旖旎浓香：指代美人。旖旎：轻盈柔美的样子。
⑦ 横斜瘦影：指梅花。化用林逋《山园小梅》："疏影横斜水清浅，暗香浮动月黄昏。"

Tune: A Sprig of Flowers

Return from the Lake

Zhang Kejiu

(I)

Rainbow clouds fall from endless sky;

Autumn's mirrored in far-flung stream.

Her rosy face looks like flower in dream,

Her flossy hair like far-off mountains green

Or colored screen.

Roadside pines in cold emerald dye,

Black brow overshadows smiling eye.

Coming with my love fair and tender,

Need I envy mume blossoms sweet and slender?

(二)梁州

挽玉手留连锦英①,

据胡床指点银瓶②。

素娥不嫁伤孤零③。

想当年小小④,

问何处卿卿。

东坡才调,

西子娉婷,

总相宜千古留名。

吾二人此地私行,

六一泉⑤亭上诗成。

① 锦英:繁华似锦。
② 银瓶:盛酒的精美器皿。
③ 孤零:孤单。
④ 小小:六朝时的钱塘名妓苏小小。
⑤ 六一泉:在西湖孤山之南,是苏轼为纪念欧阳修而命名的。欧阳修:北宋文学家,号六一居士。

(II) Tune: Song of Frontier

I linger amid flowers, holding her hand fair,

And drink in silver cup, sitting in cozy chair.

The Moon Goddess, leaving her lord, lonely appears.

I think of the young beauty without a peer.

Where is she now passing her declining years?

The brilliant talent at the height

Of his renown admired the Lady of the West

Whether richly adorned or plainly dressed.

I come here with my love at leisure,

We write verses by fountain side with pleasure.

三五夜①花前月明,
十四弦②指下风生。
可憎③,有情,
捧红牙和伊州令④。
万籁寂,
四山静,
幽咽泉流水下声⑤,
鹤怨猿惊⑥。

① 三五夜:农历十五的夜晚。
② 十四弦:古代的一种乐器。
③ 可憎:反语,极其可爱。
④ 伊州令:乐曲名。
⑤ 幽咽泉流水下声:化用白居易《琵琶行》:"幽咽泉流水下滩。"
⑥ 鹤怨猿惊:形容歌声动人心魂。

On the fifteenth night before flowers and moon bright,

Her fingers playing on fourteen strings bring a breeze light.

How lovely they seem!

Her ivory clappers accompany her song of frontier.

The night tranquil,

All mountains still,

We hear the fountain sob with running stream,

The monkey cry

And the crane sigh.

（三）尾声

岩阿禅窟鸣金磬[①]，

波底龙宫漾水精[②]。

夜色清，

酒力醒。

宝篆[③]销，

玉漏[④]鸣。

笑归来仿佛已二更，

煞强似踏雪寻梅[⑤]

灞桥冷。

① 金磬：僧人敲击的钵。
② 水精：水晶。
③ 宝篆：熏香。
④ 玉漏：古代的计时器，用铜壶滴水计时。
⑤ 煞强似踏雪寻梅：相传唐代诗人孟浩然曾在下雪天骑驴到灞桥寻梅觅诗。

(III) Tune: Epilogue

The golden bell in rocky temple rings,

The crystal palace quivers on the lake.

Night air fresh turned,

From wine I wake.

The incense burned,

Water clock sings.

When we come back in laughter, it seems midnight or after.

Is it not better than to go

To seek mume flowers on the bridge cold with snow?

凭阑人

江 夜

张可久

江水澄澄①江月明,
江上何人挡玉筝?
隔江和泪听,
满江长叹声②。

① 澄澄:清澈。
② 满江长叹声:形容筝声感人。

Tune: Leaning on Balustrade

A Night on the Stream

Zhang Kejiu

The moon shines bright on water clear.
Who's playing the lute on the stream?
It moves to tears those who hear;
Their sighs mingle with each moonbeam.

普天乐

垂虹夜月

徐再思

玉华寒,

冰壶冻。

云间玉兔,

水面苍龙①。

酒一樽,

琴三弄②。

唤起凌波仙人③梦,

倚阑干满面天风。

楼台远近,

乾坤表里,

江汉西东④。

---

① 玉华寒,冰壶冻。云间玉兔,水面苍龙:写月光照在垂虹桥上的景色。冰壶:比喻清冷的吴江。苍龙:比喻垂虹桥。
② 三弄:三支曲子。
③ 凌波仙人:曹植《洛神赋》中说他曾于洛川水边梦见洛水女神,凌波微步而来。
④ 乾坤表里,江汉西东:形容江面境界的开阔。

Tune: Universal Joy

The Moon over the Rainbow Bridge

Xu Zaisi

Cold is the moon,

Pot frozen soon.

Jade hare amid the cloud,

On water dragon proud.

A pot of wine,

Three lute songs fine

Wake up the fairy queen from her sweet dream

To tread on the waves of the stream.

I lean on rails, my face by divine breeze caressed,

Bower and tower far and nigh,

Earth and sky low and high,

And rivers east and west.

喜春来

皇亭夜泊

徐再思

水深水浅东西涧,
云去云来远近山,
秋风征棹①钓鱼滩。
烟树晚,
茅舍两三间。

① 棹:船桨。

Tune: Welcome to Spring

Mooring at Nightfall

Xu Zaisi

Water in east and west creeks are shallow or deep;
Clouds over mountains far and near come and go free.
A boat passes the fishing beach in autumn breeze.
I peep
At dusk through mist-veiled trees,
And find two thatched huts or three.

蟾宫曲

江淹①寺

徐再思

紫霜毫②是是非非,

万古虚名,

一梦初回。

失又何愁?

得之何喜?

闷也何为?

落日外萧山翠微③,

小桥边古寺残碑。

文藻珠玑,

醉墨淋漓。

何似班超,

投却毛锥④?

① 江淹:南朝人,少年时以文章著名,晚年才思减退,人称"江郎才尽"。传说江淹曾梦见前朝大诗人郭璞,要回了留在江淹手中的五色笔,从此江淹才尽。
② 紫霜毫:一种毛笔,这里指代诗文。
③ 翠微:漂浮的云气和青翠的山色。
④ 何似班超,投却毛锥:应当像班超那样,弃笔从戎,才能建立功业。毛锥,毛笔。《后汉书·班超传》记载,东汉班超靠为官府抄书来奉养母亲,有一天他喟叹道:"大丈夫没有别的智略,应当仿效傅介子、张骞立功异域来封侯,怎么能长久从事笔墨工作呢!"于是他弃文投军,后因出使西域有功,被封为定远侯。

Tune: Song of Moon Palace

Temple of a Literary Genius

Xu Zaisi

You wrote with brilliant pen on ups and downs.

It won your age-old vain renowns.

Come back from your dream,

Why at your loss should you be sad,

And at your gain be glad?

What is the use of your gloom?

Beyond the setting sun the hills appear green still,

Beside the bridge the temple ruins loom.

Your words flow like pearls in a stream;

Drunk, you spilt your ink at will.

Is it not better to be a man of men,

Who for the sword gave up the pen?

蟾宫曲

春 情

徐再思

平生不会相思,
才会相思,
便害相思。
身似浮云,
心如飞絮,
气若游丝。
空一缕余香在此,
盼千金游子何之?
证候①来时,
正是何时?
灯半昏时,
月半明时。

---

① 证候:症候,意为相思袭来。

Tune: Song of Moon Palace

Lovesickness

Xu Zaisi

In early life I knew not what lovesickness is.

When I begin to know a bit,

I fall heart and soul into a fit.

My body like cloud white,

My heart like willow down in flight,

Floating as gossamer light.

In vain a wreath of fragrance is left here.

When will my noble roamer reappear?

When comes my disease,

Can I know what time it is?

It comes by dim lamplight

When the moon is half bright.

水仙子

夜 雨

徐再思

一声梧叶一声秋,
一点芭蕉一点愁,
三更归梦三更后。
落灯花①棋未收,
叹新丰逆旅②淹留。
枕上十年事③,
江南二老④忧,
都到心头。

① 灯花:油灯上结成花形的余烬。
② 新丰逆旅:《旧唐书·马周传》记载,马周被困在新丰一事。以此来感叹自己滞留他乡。
③ 枕上十年事:躺在床上,回忆十年的往事。
④ 二老:父母。

Tune: Song of Daffodils

Rainy Night

Xu Zaisi

I hear autumn's sigh in a plane's shivering leaf;

I see raindrops on banana as drops of grief.

After midnight I dream of home-coming at midnight,

Chequers are left on chessboard by candlelight.

How can a chequered man in an inn not sigh?

Ten years like a dream on the pillow pass by.

Old parents far apart

Now come into my heart.

水仙子

春 情

徐再思

九分恩爱九分忧,
两处相思两处愁,
十年迤逗①十年受。
几遍成几遍休,
半点事半点惭羞。
三秋恨三秋感旧,
三春怨三春病酒,
一世害一世风流。

① 迤逗:挑逗。

Tune: Song of Daffodils

Love in Spring

Xu Zaisi

I am as lovesick as I'm full of care;

We long for each other here as there.

Ten years of courting give me as much joy as pain;

Our life is chequered with loss as well as gain.

There is not half a thing which brings me not half shame,

In autumn late I regret autumn flame;

In springtime fine I complain I'm sick of spring wine.

All my life long is nothing but a love song.

人月圆

甘露怀古

徐再思

江皋楼观前朝寺,
秋色入秦淮。
败垣① 芳草,
空廊落叶,
深砌苍苔。
远人南去,
夕阳西下,
江水东来。
木兰花在,
山僧试问,
知为谁开?

① 垣:矮墙。

Tune: Man and Moon

The Ancient Temple of Sweet Dew

Xu Zaisi

By riverside stands ancient Temple of Sweet Dew,

Invaded by autumn hue.

Ruined walls overgrown with wild grass,

Empty gallery paved with fallen leaves, alas!

Oldened steps covered with moss green.

No more tourists are seen.

Down in the west the sun goes,

The river to the east flows.

Only the magnolia blows.

I ask the monk for whom,

The flowers are in bloom.

朝天子

西　湖

徐再思

里湖,
外湖,
无处是无春处。
真山真水真画图,
一片玲珑玉。
宜酒宜诗,
宜晴宜雨。
销金锅
锦绣窟,
老苏①,
老逋②,
杨柳堤梅花墓。

---

① 老苏：北宋诗人苏轼，曾为杭州太守，在西湖建苏堤，堤上多杨柳。
② 老逋：北宋诗人林逋，曾隐居西湖孤山，号称"梅妻鹤子"。

Tune: Skyward Song
West Lake

Xu Zaisi

In inner lake

And outer lake,

There's nowhere but spring is awake.

True hills and water make the picture true,

No carved jade can outdo.

It's good for verse and for wine,

Rain or shine.

It is a place where gold may be spent,

And brocade used as ornament.

Oh! Poet Su,

Mume-lover Bu,

You might still find your willows' gloom

And flowers' tomb.

一半儿

春 妆

查德卿

自将杨柳品题人,
笑拈花枝比较春①,
输与海棠三四分。
再偷匀,
一半儿胭脂一半儿粉。

---

① 自将杨柳品题人,笑拈花枝比较春:少女将自己的美貌与春日的杨柳、花枝做比较的娇憨模样。

Tune: Half and Half

Spring Attire

Zha Deqing

She tries to compare herself with the willow tree,
And holds a twig to see which reveals vernal glee.
Finding herself less lovely than crab-apple flower,
Again she makes up in her bower,
Powders her face and rouges her lips with grace.

柳营曲

金陵^①故址

查德卿

临故国,

认残碑,

伤心六朝如逝水。

物换星移,

城是人非,

今古一枰棋。

南柯梦一觉初回,

北邙坟^②三尺荒堆。

四围山护绕,

几处树高低。

谁

曾赋黍离离^③?

---

① 金陵：南京，为六朝古都。
② 北邙坟：邙山在河南洛阳市东北，汉朝以来，许多王公贵族埋葬于此，北邙山泛指墓地。
③ 黍离离：《诗经·黍离》有："彼黍离离，彼稷之苗。行迈靡靡，中心摇摇。知我者谓我心忧，不知我者谓我何求。"这是抒发亡国之痛的名篇，黍离也就成为亡国之恨的代名词。黍：谷物的名称。离离：成排成行的样子。

Tune: Song of Willow Camp

The Ancient Capital at Jinling

Zha Deqing

Coming to ancient capital,

I find nothing but ruined wall,

Grieved that Six Dynasties have passed like running stream.

Things have changed and stars turned around;

Men live not so long as towns stand.

History is nothing less than a game of chess.

Soon we wake up from our vain dream

To find on northern land but burial mound,

Which mountains on four sides surround.

How many trees grow

High and low?

Who is grieved over the waste land!

一枝花

唐毅夫

（一）怨雪

不呈六出[①]祥，
岂应三白瑞[②]？
易添身上冷，
能使腹中饥。
有甚稀奇？
无主向沿街坠，
不着人到处飞。
暗敲窗有影无形，
偷入门潜踪蹑迹。

[①] 六出：雪花有六个瓣，故称"六出"。
[②] 三白瑞：古人认为正月里下三次雪，来年庄稼收成就好。

Tune: A Sprig of Flowers

Tang Yifu

(I) Complaint Against Snow

Is snow of any good?
No bumper year's foretold.
It brings the poor no food
But makes the hungry cold
As of old.
Aimless, it falls along the street;
Carefree, it flies to any place.
It knocks on window-panes with unseen feet,
And steals indoors without leaving trace.

（二）梁州

才苫上①茅庵草舍，

又钻入破壁疏篱，

似杨花滚滚轻狂②势。

俺几曾③见贵公子锦裀绣褥？

你多曾伴老渔翁箬笠蓑衣？

为飘风胡作胡为，

怕腾云相趁相随。

只着你冻的个孟浩然挣挣痴痴，

只着你逼的个林和靖钦钦历历，

只着你阻的个韩退之哭哭啼啼④。

---

① 苫上：编茅盖屋。
② 轻狂：轻浮癫狂。
③ 几曾：何曾。
④ 只着你阻的个韩退之哭哭啼啼：孟浩然被你冻得缩手缩脚，林和靖被你逼得哆哆嗦嗦，韩愈被你拦住去路，急得直哭。

(II) Tune: Song of Frontier

You cling to thatched cot,

And pierce into leaky wall,

Frivolous as wave on wave of willow down.

Have you ever been close to noble son's gown

Or quilt of brocade light,

Or kept company with fishermen old

In straw cloak and hat of bamboo?

You do what you will with the wind roaring loud

In company with heavy cloud.

You care not for the poet frozen on his ass,

Not knowing what to do;

Nor the mume-lover Lin Bu

Shivering with cold;

Nor the banished scholar barred on his way

At the Blue Pass.

更长,
漏迟,
被窝中无半点儿阳和气①。
恼人眠搅人睡,
你那冷燥皮肤似铁石,
着我怎敢相偎?

① 阳和气:暖和气。

Long lasts the night;

Late breaks the day.

My poor quilt is not,

Not warmed at all.

How can I fall asleep

Even when night is deep?

Your skin is cold and hard as iron or stone.

How dare I cling to you alone?

（三）尾

一冬酒债因他累，
千里关山被你①迷。
似这等浪蕊②闲花
也不是长久计。
尽飘零数日，
扫除做一堆，
我将你温不热薄情儿
化做了水。

---

① 他、你：都指雪。
② 浪蕊：雪花。

(III) Tune: Epilogue

All winter long I am in heavy debt for wine.

I can't go home for you've barred my way for miles and miles.

You fruitless flower, can you last for years?

Though you may wander from day to day,

At last I will sweep you away

And heap you up into piles.

Cold as you are, when the day is fine,

I'll warm you up and dissolve you into tears.

天净沙

秋

朱庭玉

庭前落尽梧桐,
水边开彻①芙蓉。
解与诗人意同②,
辞柯霜叶,
飞来就我题红③。

① 开彻:开过,要凋零了。
② 解与诗人意同:指凋零的梧桐叶与荷花似乎与诗人心意相通。
③ 辞柯霜叶,飞来就我题红:这是诗人在向飘落的树叶说话;经过秋霜离开树枝的落叶啊,飞到我身边吧,我将在你上面用红笔写下诗句。

Tune: Sunny Sand

Autumn

Zhu Tingyu

In the courtyard the leafless plane trees loom;
By waterside all lotuses are in full bloom.
The frost-bitten maple leaf knows my heart,
Willing from its bough to part
And fly down for me to write verses on.

普天乐

咏 世

张鸣善

洛阳花,
梁园月,
好花须买,
皓月须赊[①]。
花倚栏杆看烂漫开,
月曾把酒问团圆夜。
月有盈亏花有开谢,
想人生最苦离别。
花谢了三春近也,
月缺了中秋到也,
人去了何日来也?

① 赊:借钱买。

Tune: Universal Joy

Apart in the World

Zhang Mingshan

O peony flowers!

O moonlit bowers!

Bright flowers can be bought when they are desired;

Bright moon cannot be brought down when admired.

You may see full-blown flowers from the balustrade,

And drink to the full moon when you gather round.

The moon may wax and wane, flowers may bloom or fade.

What gnaws our heart is to be torn apart.

Faded flowers may blow again when spring comes around;

The waning moon may wax full on Mid-autumn Day.

O when will you come back now you are far away?

普天乐

愁 怀

张鸣善

雨儿飘,

风儿扬。

风吹回好梦,

雨滴损柔肠。

风萧萧梧叶中,

雨点点芭蕉上。

风雨相留添悲怆,

雨和风卷起凄凉。

风雨儿怎当?

风雨儿定当,

风雨儿难当[①]!

[①] 风雨儿怎当? 风雨儿定当, 风雨儿难当: 风雨交加, 我怎么过啊? 但是不论我怎么样, 风雨还是依旧。风雨交加, 真是难熬啊!

Tune: Universal Joy

Grief at Heart

Zhang Mingshan

Wind roars;

Rain pours.

Wind tears my dream apart;

Rain breaks my tender heart.

Wind soughs in gales among plane trees;

Rain falls drop on drop on banana leaves.

Wind accompanied with rain grieves;

Rain saddens, rolled up by dreary breeze.

How can I bear wind and rain?

Whatever I do, they remain.

I'd bear them now and again.

普天乐

嘲西席[1]

张鸣善

讲诗书,
习功课。
爹娘行[2]孝顺,
兄弟行谦和。
为臣要尽忠,
与朋友休言过[3]。
养性终朝端然坐,
免教人笑俺风魔。
先生道学生琢磨,
学生道先生絮聒[4],
馆东[5]道不识字由他。

---

[1] 西席:古人以坐西面东为客位,教书先生常被称为西席或西宾。
[2] 行:面前,那里。
[3] 休言过:不要说别人的过错。
[4] 絮聒:啰唆。
[5] 馆东:书馆主人。

Tune: Universal Joy

To a Funny Tutor

Zhang Mingshan

You teach pupils to read and write,

And they learn to recite,

To obey their fathers and mothers,

To be good towards their brothers,

To serve their prince to the end,

And not to find fault with their friend.

Well bred, you make a pose all the day long,

Lest people should say you are wrong.

You tell the pupils: "Your work should be well done."

But they say: "The work is a tedious one."

And the father says: "All is up to my son."

水仙子

西湖探梅

杨朝英

雪晴天地一冰壶,
竟往西湖探老逋[①],
骑驴踏雪溪桥路[②]。
笑王维作画图[③],
拣梅花多处提壶。
对酒看花笑,
无钱当剑沽,
醉倒在西湖。

---

① 老逋：北宋诗人林逋，曾隐居西湖孤山，他酷爱梅花，在居所周围种了许多梅树。这里以老逋指代梅花。
② 骑驴踏雪溪桥路：唐代诗人孟浩然曾在雪天骑驴到霸桥赏梅花。
③ 笑王维作画图：王维画有《雪溪图》，诗人感叹西湖雪景远胜过王维的画。

Tune: Song of Daffodils

Mume Blossoms at West Lake

Yang Chaoying

The sky and earth look like icy pot after snow.
To seek after mume blossoms in West Lake I go.
Treading on snow by the brook on an ass I ride,
I've outdone the poet's picture of the lakeside.
I bring a pot of wine where mume blossoms throng;
Wine cup in hand, I smile at the flowers for long.
Wine drunk up, I may pawn my sword to buy;
Drunk down, by lakeside I would lie.

山坡羊

道 情

宋方壶

青山相待,

白云相爱,

梦不到紫罗袍共黄金带[①]。

一茅斋,

野花开,

管甚谁家兴废谁成败?

陋巷箪瓢[②]亦乐哉!

贫,气不改;

达,志不改[③]。

---

① 紫罗袍、黄金带:官服,代指做官。
② 陋巷箪瓢:典故出自《论语·雍也》,孔子称赞颜回安贫乐道:"一箪食,一瓢饮,在陋巷,人不堪其忧,回也不改其乐。"
③ 贫,气不改;达,志不改:意谓贫贱不能移,富贵不能淫的操守。

Tune: Sheep on the Slope

A Carefree Dream

Song Fanghu

Blue hills greet and love me

With white clouds above me.

I do not dream of golden belt or violet dress,

But of a thatched room

With wild flowers in bloom,

Careless alike of rise and fall, of failure and success.

In simple food and plain living I'll find delight.

Of poverty I would make light;

Success can't raise me to the height.

清江引

托 咏

宋方壶

剔①秃圞②一轮天外月,
拜了低低说:
是必③常团圆,
休着些儿④缺。
愿天下有情底都似你者⑤。

① 剔:忒,特别。
② 秃圞:圆圆的样子。
③ 是必:一定。
④ 些儿:一点点。
⑤ 者:语助词,表示祈使。

Tune: Song of Clear River

To the Moon

Song Fanghu

So round is the full moon in the sky.

I bow and whisper to her in view:

"You must be forever round on high,

And never wane to the eye!

I wish that those in love shall gather round as you."

斗鹌鹑

送 别

宋方壶

（一）

落日遥岑①，
淡烟远浦②。
萧寺③疏钟，
戍楼暮鼓。
一叶扁舟，
数声去橹。
那惨戚，
那凄楚，
恰待欢娱，
顿成间阻。

---

① 岑：小而高的山。
② 浦：小河流入江海的入口处。
③ 萧寺：佛寺。梁武帝萧衍造佛寺，命人书曰"萧寺"，后世即用以指代佛寺。

Tune: Fight of Quails

Parting

Song Fanghu

(I)

At sunset stretch out disant hills

And far-flung mist-veiled rills,

But few temple bells ring

With drumbeats watch-towers bring.

A leaflike boat

Rows away and afloat.

How drear and sad

Our parting song!

Our short meeting so glad,

Our separation so long!

(二)紫花儿

瘦岩岩香消玉减,

冷清清夜永更长,

孤零零枕剩衾余。

羞花闭月,

落雁沉鱼。

踌躇,

从今后谁寄萧娘一纸书[①]?

无情无绪,

水淹蓝桥[②],

梦断华胥[③]。

---

① 萧娘一纸书:唐人杨巨源《崔娘》诗:"风流才子多春思,肠断萧娘一纸书。"这里用典故含蓄地表达了肝肠寸断的相思之情。
② 水淹蓝桥:传说战国时鲁人尾生与女子约会桥下,女子没来,河水却在上涨,尾生坚守约定留在原处,最后抱着桥柱被水淹死。经过后代演绎,蓝桥成为情人相会之所的代称,水淹蓝桥指夫妻分离或情人不能相见。
③ 华胥:传说上古时皇帝白天睡觉,梦见周游华胥之国,那里没有一切不平等和丑恶,是个完美的理想国。

(II) Tune: Violet Flowers

My slender, slender body wastes away;

The chilly, chilly nights longer stay.

In lonely, lonely bed warmth is worn out.

Will the moon and flowers feel shy at my sight,

And wild geese and fish take flight?

I doubt.

From now on who will send a letter to me?

I fade without glee.

The blue bridge is drowned in the stream

When I awake from my sweet dream.

（三）调笑令

肺腑，

恨怎舒？

三叠阳关愁万缕，

幽期密约欢爱处，

动离愁暮云无数。

今夜月明何处宿①？

依依古岸黄芦。

---

① 今夜月明何处宿：化用柳永《雨霖铃》："今宵酒醒何处，杨柳岸晓风残月。"

(III) Tune: Song of Flirtation

How to give relief

To my heart-felt grief?

The farewell song with three refrains heard,

My thousand threads of sorrow stirred,

I'm grieved to see countless evening clouds above,

They remind me of where we were happy in love.

Where will you moor your boat in the moonlight?

Are you missing me by the reedy shore tonight?

(四)秃厮儿

欢笑地不堪举目,
回首处景物萧疏。
屋前月下谁共语?
漫嗟吁①,
自踌躇
何如?

---

① 嗟吁:叹息。

(IV) Tune: The Bald Head

I dare not raise the eye

To places of delight.

Looking back, I find gloomy our rendezvous.

With whom could I talk in moonlight and starlight?

What can I do

But walk back and forth

And give sigh on sigh?

（五）圣药王

别太速，

情最苦。

松①金减玉瘦了身躯。

鬼病添，

神思虚，

心如刀剜泪如珠。

意儿里懒上香车。

① 松：松动，减少。

(V) Tune: Sovereign of Medicine

Do not make haste!

The bitterest grief makes my jade-like body waste,

My illness more severe,

My head less clear,

And gnaws my heart till my pearl-like tears fall.

So idle and so drear,

I would not mount my fragrant cab at all.

（六）尾

眼睁睁怎忍分飞去?
痛杀我也吹箫伴侣。
不付能①恰住了送行客一帆风。
又添起助离愁半江雨。

① 不付能：好不容易。

(VI) Tune: Epilogue

How can I bear with open eyes to see us part?
To leave my flute companion would break my heart.
Hardly have I not heard the wind to say goodbye,
When grievous rain makes half the river run high.

醉高歌过红绣鞋

寄金莺儿[①]

贾　固

（一）醉高歌

乐心儿比目连枝，
肯意儿新婚燕尔。
画船开抛闪的人独自，
遥望关西[②]店儿。
黄河水流不尽心事，
中条山隔不断相思。

[①] 金莺儿：当时的山东名妓，元人夏庭芝《青楼记》有对她的记载。
[②] 关西：函谷关以西。贾固曾任"西台御史"，赴任道中经过关西店儿。

From "Drinking Song" to "Embroidered Red Shoes"

For Golden Oriole

Jia Gu

(I) Tune: Drinking Song

Like flatfish or twin branches of a tree,

We were as happy as a pair of swallows free.

My parting boat left you alone on shore, alas!

Gazing as far as west of the Sunny Pass.

Our love like Yellow River keeps on flowing;

The Middle Mountain can't bar it from growing.

(二)红绣鞋

当记得夜深沉,
人静悄,
自来时①。
来时节三两句话,
去时节一篇诗,
记在人心窝儿里直到死。

---

① 当记得夜深沉,人静悄,自来时:回忆他们初次见面时的情景。

(II) Tune: Embroidered Red Shoes

Remember when night was deep,

All fell asleep,

You came alone.

Come, you spoke but two words or three;

Gone, you got a verse from me,

It would be kept at heart till we are dead and gone.

塞鸿秋

浔阳①即景

周德清

长江万里白如练②,

淮山③数点青如淀。

江帆几片疾如箭,

山泉千尺飞如电。

晚云都变露④,

新月初学扇⑤。

塞鸿⑥一字来如线。

---

① 浔阳:今江西九江市,其北有浔阳江。
② 练:白色的丝织品。化用谢朓《晚登三山还望京邑》:"余霞散成绮,澄江静如练。"
③ 淮山:淮河流域的山脉。淀:通"靛",是一种深蓝色的染料。
④ 晚云都变露:晚霞消失,夜幕降临。
⑤ 新月初学扇:新月就像一把半圆形的团扇。
⑥ 塞鸿:塞外南飞的大雁。

Tune: Autumn Swan on Frontier

By the River of Xunyang

Zhou Deqing

For miles and miles the endless river flows silk-white;

Dots on dots of southern hills stand indigo-blue.

Sails on sails go past as fast arrows do;

The waterfall dashes down like lightning from the height.

All evening clouds turn into dew;

The crescent moon imitates a bow;

The wild geese from the frontier fly in a row.

满庭芳

看岳王传

周德清

披文握武①,
建中兴庙宇②。
载青史图书③。
功成却被权臣妒,
正落奸谋④。
闪杀人望旌节中原士夫⑤;
误杀人弃丘陵南渡銮舆⑥。
钱塘⑦路,
愁风怨雨,
长是洒西湖。

① 披文握武:指岳飞兼有文武之才。
② 建中兴庙宇:建立了中兴的事业。庙宇:宗庙社稷。
③ 载青史图书:指岳飞的抗金事迹被载入史册。
④ 功成却被权臣妒,正落奸谋:指岳飞大破金兵于朱仙镇,本可以进一步收复失地,但当时主和派的秦桧召岳飞还朝,诬陷岳飞入狱。
⑤ 闪杀人望旌节中原士夫:南宋的统治者抛弃了中原,偏安江南,而中原的人民日夜盼望恢复。闪杀人:害死人。旌节:朝廷使臣的符节。士夫:泛指人民。
⑥ 銮舆:天子的车驾。
⑦ 钱塘:南宋临安,今杭州。

Tune: Courtyard Full of Fragrance

On the Tomb of General Yue

Zhou Deqing

By word and sword he tried

To rebuild the royal temple's fame,

And left in history an undying name.

But envied by traitors before he had won,

He was treacherously slain,

Leaving unrecovered the lost Central Plain,

And Northern royal tombs not visited again.

His work undone,

The dreary wind and drizzling rain

Are weeping for the General buried by lake side.

折桂令

周德清

倚蓬窗^①无语嗟呀,

七件儿^②全无,

做甚么人家?

柴似灵芝,

油如甘露,

米若丹砂^③。

酱瓮儿才罄撒^④,

盐瓶儿又告消乏。

茶也无多,

醋也无多。

七件事尚且艰难,

怎生教我折柳攀花^⑤!

---

① 蓬窗:茅舍的窗户。
② 七件儿:俗称柴、米、油、盐、酱、醋、茶为"开门七件事"。
③ 灵芝、甘露、丹砂:都是名贵的药材。此处用以比喻物价太高。
④ 罄撒:缺乏、短少,与下句的"消乏"同意。
⑤ 折柳攀花:指狎妓,泛指优游荒唐的生活。

Tune: Plucking Laurel Branch

Zhou Deqing

Leaning on windowsill, speechless I sigh.
Without the seven necessities,
How could households be called families?
The fuel is as dear as wood cut from on high,
Oil as nectar of dew,
And rice as pearls all new.
The sauce is used up in the jar,
The salt bottle is empty, you see,
There's no more tea,
Nor vinegar.
I can hardly afford these seven necessities,
How could I enjoy flowers and willow trees?

一枝花

秋夜闻筝

班惟志

（一）

透疏帘风摇杨柳阴，
泻长空月转梧桐影。
冷雕盘香销金兽①火，
咽铜龙②漏滴玉壶冰。
何处银筝？
声嘹呖③云霄应，
逐轻风过短棂④，
耳才闻天上仙乐，
身疑在人间胜境。

---

① 金兽：金属做的兽形小手炉。
② 铜龙：古人以铜壶滴漏计时，壶嘴滴水处饰以龙嘴，叫作铜龙。
③ 嘹呖：嘹亮，响亮。
④ 逐轻风过短棂：筝声随风传来，像鸟儿一样追逐着清风，飘进了窗棂。短棂：小窗户。

Tune: A Sprig of Flowers

The Zither Heard on an Autumn Night

Ban Weizhi

(I)

On window screen the breeze sways shadows of willow trees;

In wide sky the moon round casts plane's shade on the ground.

On chiseled plate of gold incense is burned and cold;

The bronze dragon sobs when icy waterclock throbs.

From where comes the zither song?

It's echoed loud and clear among the clouds for long.

It wafts with the light breeze far and near.

The divine music has just reached my ear,

My body seems to float in celestial sphere.

（二）梁州

恰便似溅石窟寒泉乱涌，

集瑶台鸾凤和鸣，

走金盘乱撒骊珠①迸。

嘶风骏偃，潜沼鱼惊。

天边雁落，树梢云停②。

早则是字样分明，更哪堪音律关情？

凄凉比汉昭君塞上琵琶，

清韵如王子乔③风前玉笙，

悠扬似张君瑞④月下琴声。

再听，愈惊。

叮咛一曲《阳关令》。

感离愁，动别兴。

万事萦怀百样增，一洗尘清。

① 骊珠：珍珠。
② 嘶风骏偃，潜沼鱼惊。天边雁落，树梢云停：用四个夸张句表现筝声的美妙：它使骏马停止了奔腾，使深水中的鱼儿惊觉起来，使高飞的大雁从天边掉落，使飘游的云朵在树梢停留。
③ 王子乔：神话人物，喜吹笙作凤鸣声，后得到仙人指点，修炼升仙。
④ 张君瑞：《西厢记》中的张生，在月夜弹琴来向崔莺莺表达爱慕。

(II) Tune: Song of Frontier

It's like cold fountain splashing on the stone,
Phoenix and pheasant singing in the moon,
Or pearls rolling in plate of gold.
It stops the steed running in wind so cold,
Startles the fish swimming in the pond
And wild geese flying on horizon and beyond,
And detains the cloud floating atop the trees.
Its word on word is clearly heard.
How can we bear its heart-rending tune?
It's drear as the Princess' lament on the frontier,
Clear as the Prince playing on his jade flute,
Melodious as the lover's moonlit lute.
Listen again and you will be startled anew,
It is the song of Sunny Pass bidding adieu.
You will be grieved to hear the lovers say goodbye,
All hidden in your heart would burst into a sigh.
All dust washed away, what care have you?

(三)尾

她那里轻笼纤指冰弦应①,
俺这里慢写花笺锦字迎。
越感起文园少年病。
是谁家玉卿?
只恁般可憎②!
唤的人一枕蝴蝶梦儿醒。

---

① 她那里轻笼纤指冰弦应:诗人展开了想象——弹筝之人一定是位玉指轻拢冰弦的美人。
② 可憎:可爱,惹人怜惜。

(III) Tune: Epilogue

Her fair fingers lightly touch the icy strings;
I'd write to her a letter interwoven with flowers,
Remembering the young writer in his bowers.
Who can be this lover of springs?
O why so lovely should she be!
Her song sinks me into and wakens me
From my dream of butterfly on the wings.

醉太平

警 世

汪元亨

憎苍蝇竞血,
恶黑蚁争穴。
急流中勇退是豪杰。
不因循苟且①,
叹乌衣一旦非王谢②,
怕青山两岸分吴越③,
厌红尘万丈混龙蛇④,
老先生去也⑤。

① 因循苟且：循规蹈矩，得过且过。
② 叹乌衣一旦非王谢：嗟叹富贵转眼成空。乌衣：指乌衣巷，晋代王谢家族住居的地方，后来就衰落了。
③ 怕青山两岸分吴越：害怕争雄竞霸的斗争。春秋时期吴越两国山水相接，经常发生争斗，后来吴国为越国所灭。
④ 厌红尘万丈混龙蛇：厌恶尘世的纷扰。红尘：指污浊的社会。混龙蛇：贤愚相混。
⑤ 老先生去也：指自己即将急流勇退，远离世俗。

Tune: Drunk in Time of Peace

Disgust with the World

Wang Yuanheng

I hate flies striving to suck blood,

And black ants fighting for food.

A brave man will retire at the high tide,

And not follow the old rut or drift along.

I sigh for mansions to lords no longer belong,

And fear blue hills into hostile states divide.

I dislike dragons mingling with snakes in the dust.

As an old man, I'll leave them with disgust.

朝天子

归 隐

汪元亨

荣华梦一场,

功名纸半张,

是非海波千丈。

马蹄踏碎禁街①霜,

听几度头鸡唱②。

尘土衣冠,

江湖心量③,

出皇家麟凤网④。

慕夷齐首阳⑤,

叹韩彭⑥未央⑦,

早纳纸风魔状⑧。

① 禁街:宫廷中的道路。
② 头鸡唱:头遍鸡叫,指天亮前起床。
③ 心量:胸怀,气度。
④ 麟凤网:指皇家控制大臣的罗网。
⑤ 夷齐首阳:周武王时,伯夷、叔齐不食周粟,隐居首阳山中,被后人看作是隐居的楷模。
⑥ 韩彭:韩信、彭越,他们都是辅佐刘邦夺得天下的功臣,汉初被封为诸侯王,后被告发谋反,先后被处死。
⑦ 未央:未央宫,这里指韩信、彭越丧身的地方。
⑧ 状:文书。

Tune: Skyward Song

Hermitage

Wang Yuanheng

Glory is but a dream,

Rank and fame paper torn,

Right or wrong mountain-high tide.

Why should my horse have trod frosty royal streets down?

How many times have I heard cocks crow at dawn?

All cloaks and crowns will be outworn.

Why not retire on the lake or the stream?

Why fall into the royal snare of renown?

I'd like to be hermit by the hillside.

Pitying heroes slain in palace sad.

I'd rather resign or pretend to be mad.

沉醉东风

归 田

汪元亨

远城市人稠物穰,
近村居水色山光。
熏陶成野叟情,
铲削去时官样,
演习会牧歌樵唱。
老瓦盆边醉几场,
不撞入天罗地网。

Tune: Intoxicated in East Wind

Return to My Field

Wang Yuanheng

I'd live far from the crowded market town,

and near green hills and blue rills up and down.

Cultivated into a wild man with hair grey,

I'd get rid of modern official way,

And learn to sing a shepherd's or woodman's song.

Drunk all day long,

Beside my earthenwares,

I would not fall into the mundane snares.

人月圆

倪 瓒

惊回一枕当年梦,
渔唱起南津。
画屏云嶂①,
池塘春草,
无限销魂。
旧家应在,
梧桐覆井,
杨柳藏门。
闲身②空老,
孤篷听雨,
灯火江村。

① 画屏云嶂:屏风上画着云和山。
② 闲身:清闲之身。

Tune: Man and Moon

Ni Zan

Startled on my pillow from my dream

Of bygone years by fishing song at southern stream,

I see peak on peak veiled in clouds like a screen,

And pool on pool seem overgrown with grass green.

How much it grieves

My heart to think of my house of yore

Overshadowed by plane leaves.

With doors hidden amid willow trees.

At ease,

I am oldened in vain.

What can I do but listen to the rain

Or see flickering lights on river shore?

小桃红

倪 瓒

一江秋水澹寒烟[①],
水影明如练。
眼底离愁数行雁。
雪晴天,
绿苹红蓼参差见。
吴歌[②]荡桨,
一声哀怨,
惊起白鸥眠。

---

① 澹寒烟:水面上薄薄的雾气。
② 吴歌:江南地区的民歌。

Tune: Red Peach Blossoms

Ni Zan

On autumn stream pale smoke and cold mist rise,

With water crystal-clear and silk-white.

A few rows of wild geese bring parting grief to the eyes.

After snow the sunny sky's bright,

Green duckweed and red knotweed high and low appear.

The rower sings a Southern song on the stream,

So plaintive and so drear,

A white gull's startled from its dream.

凭阑人
赠吴国良①

倪 瓒

客有吴郎吹洞箫,
明月沉江春雾晓。
湘灵②不可招,
水云中环佩摇。

① 吴国良:倪瓒的好友,即曲中所说的吴郎,史料记载他工制墨、善吹箫,好与贤士大夫游。
② 湘灵:一般指舜的两位妃子娥皇和女英;此外,我国神话传说中有"琴箫湘瑟"之说,琴箫指秦代善于吹箫的箫史,湘瑟源于楚辞《远游》:"使湘灵鼓瑟兮"之句。

Tune: Leaning on Balustrade

For A Friend

Ni Zan

My friend is good at playing on the flute green,

It may bring down the moon on misty stream in spring.

Why can it not attract the fairy queen?

In cloud and water you may hear jade pendants ring.

水仙子

倪 瓒

东风花外小红楼①,
南浦②山横眉黛愁。
春寒不管花枝瘦,
无情水自流。
檐间燕语娇柔,
惊回幽梦,
难寻旧游,
落日帘钩。

① 红楼:古代一般指女子的住处。
② 南浦:《楚辞·九歌》有:"送美人兮南浦。"南浦因此被后人用来指代送别之地。

Tune: Song of Daffodils

Ni Zan

The east wind can't bring flower to her small red bower;
The mountains bar the sky like eyebrows in green dye.
The cold spring cares not of the slender blooming tree,
The heartless water flows away, carefree.
A pair of tender swallows whisper on the beam,
Awaking her from her sweet dream.
Where can she find her lover? Look!
The setting sun seems to hang on the curtain's hook.

折桂令

忆 别

刘庭信

想人生最苦离别,

唱到阳关,

休唱三叠①。

急煎煎抹泪柔眵②,

意迟迟揉腮撅耳③,

呆答孩④闭口藏舌。

情儿分儿你心里记者⑤,

病儿痛儿我身上添些,

家儿活儿既是抛撇,

书儿信儿是必休绝,

花儿草儿打听的风声,

车儿马儿我亲自来也⑥!

① 唱到阳关,休唱三叠:唐代王维有《送元二使安西》:"渭城朝雨浥清尘,客舍青青柳色新。劝君更尽一杯酒,西出阳关无故人。"它被后人谱乐歌唱,最后一句反复歌唱三遍,称为《阳关三叠》,是送别的经典曲目。
② 柔眵:擦眼睛。眵:眼屎。
③ 揉腮撅耳:挠腮挖耳,不耐烦的样子。
④ 呆答孩:呆呆的样子。
⑤ 记者:记住。
⑥ 花儿草儿打听的风声,车儿马儿我亲自来也:如果打听到你拈花惹草的消息,我就要骑着马儿来和你算账。

Tune: Plucking Laurel Branch

Parting Recalled

Liu Tingxin

Parting's the greatest grief in life, alas!
Don't sing thrice the refrain
Of farewell song of Sunny Pass!
Worried to death, I wipe away my tears;
At a loss, I stroke my chin and ears;
Stupified, I shut my mouth tongue-tied.
My love for you, you should keep in heart;
Of ill and pain I would bear my part.
Of household work, you need not care a grain.
But don't forget to bring me word now and again!
If I know you are in love with another flower,
At once in cab and horse I'll leave my bower.

水仙子

相　思

刘庭信

恨重叠,

重叠恨,

恨绵绵,

恨满晚妆楼。

愁积聚,

积聚愁,

愁切切,

愁斟碧玉瓯。

懒梳妆,

梳妆懒,

懒设设,

懒爇①黄金兽。

泪珠弹,

弹泪珠,

泪汪汪,

汪汪不住流。

① 爇：点燃。

Tune: Song of Daffodils

Lovesickness

Liu Tingxin

Oh, deep regret

On regret deep

I can't forget!

At dusk it overwhelms my bower and I weep.

Piled-up sorrow,

Sorrow piled-up,

Sorrow lasts till the morrow,

It drinks my blood in emerald cup.

I am idle,

Idle am I,

Made up, I would sidle;

Incense burned, I would sigh.

I shed tears,

Tears are shed,

My face appears,

Tearful as if with water overspread.

病身躯,
身躯病,
病恹恹,
病在我心头。
花见我,
我见花,
花应憔瘦。
月对咱,
咱对月,
月更害羞。
与天说,
说与天,
天也还愁。

I am ill,

Ill am I,

Languid still,

My heart would utter cry on cry.

I see the bloom,

The bloom sees me,

Languid and lean she'd also be.

I and the moon,

The moon and I,

Looking in my face, she'd feel shy.

I ask the sky soon,

It won't reply,

For like me it's also in deep gloom.

一枝花

春日送别

刘庭信

丝丝杨柳风,
点点梨花雨。
雨随花瓣落,
风趁柳条疏。
春事成虚,
无奈春归去。
春归何太速?
试问东君①:
谁肯与莺花做主?

① 东君:司春之神。

Tune: A Sprig of Flowers

Farewell to Spring

Liu Tingxin

Thread by thread willow twigs sway in the breeze,

Drop on drop falls the rain on pear trees.

Pear petals fall with the rain,

The wind goes down with willow down.

Springtime has passed in vain.

What can I do when it has passed?

Why has it gone so fast?

I ask the Eastern Lord in power,

Who cares for wailing bird and weeping flower?

小梁州

九日渡江

汤 式

（一）

秋风江上棹孤舟，

烟水悠悠。

伤心无句赋登楼，

山容瘦，

老树替人愁。

（幺）

樽前醉把茱萸嗅，

问相知几个白头[①]？

乐可酬，

人非旧，

黄花时候，

难比旧风流。

[①] 樽前醉把茱萸嗅，问相知几个白头：化用杜甫《九日蓝田崔氏庄》诗句："明年此会知谁健，醉把茱萸仔细看。"

Tune: Minor Frontier

Crossing the River on Mountain-climbing Day

Tang Shi

(I)

I sail a lonely boat on the stream in autumn breeze,

The misty water runs without cease.

Heart-broken, I have no verse to write on tower high.

Lean mountains seem to sigh,

Like me are grieved old trees.

When drunk before my cup, I smell at dogwood spray,

Asking how many friends have their heads turned grey.

I may seek pleasure again,

But friends are not the same as then.

When yellow flowers bloom once more,

Who would enjoy with me their beauty as of yore?

（二）

秋风江上棹孤航，

烟水茫茫。

白云西去雁南翔，

推篷望，

清思满沧浪。

（幺）

东篱载酒陶元亮[①]，

等闲[②]间过了重阳。

自感伤，

何情况，

黄花惆怅，

空作去年香。

---

① 陶元亮：陶渊明，元亮是他的字。
② 等闲：平常，随便。

(II)

In autumn breeze my lonely boat sails on the stream,

Boundless the mist and water seem.

White clouds westward go

While wild geese southward fly,

I open the window, lo!

The waves with my thoughts surge up high.

Like poet Tao I'd drink before flowers in bloom,

Wasting my time on Mountain-climbing Day.

So sad and drear,

How can I not waste away?

The chrysanthemums are also in gloom,

In vain they smell sweet as last year.

天香引

忆维扬[①]

汤 式

羡江都自古神州,

天上人间,

楚尾吴头[②]。

十万家画栋朱帘,

百数曲红桥绿沼,

三千里锦缆龙舟。

柳招摇,花掩映,

春风紫骝。

玉玎珰,

珠络索,

夜月香兜[③]。

歌舞都休,

光景难留。

富贵随落日西沉,

繁华逐逝水东流。

[①] 维扬:扬州的别称。
[②] 楚尾吴头:出自宋人《江庭怨》词:"泪眼不曾晴,家住吴头楚尾。"意为扬州的地理位置在楚国和吴国的交界。
[③] 兜:同"篼",是一种轻便的竹轿子。

Tune: Song of Celestial Fragrance

Riverside Town Recalled

Tang Shi

How I adore the capital on rivershore!
It was an earthly paradise,
With eastern head and southern end so nice.
Thousands of homes with painted beam and pearly screen,
Hundreds of winding bridges over water green,
Embroidered dragon boats for miles and miles overspread.
Along the swaying willow trees,
Among the blooming flowers red,
The violet steeds were running in the vernal breeze.
With ringing pendants of jade
And pearls and earrings bright,
The fragrant sedans vied in beauty with moonlight.
No more dance and songs in light or shade,
None could retain good times of yore.
Magnificence has gone with the declining day;
Splendor like running water has passed away.

四块玉

风 情

兰楚芳

（一）

意思儿真，
心肠儿顺。
只争个口角头不囫囵①。
怕人知，
羞人说，
嗔②人问。
不见后又嗔，
得见后又忖，
多敢死后背。

① 囫囵：糊涂，不清楚。
② 嗔：生气。

Tune: Four Pieces of Jade

A Maid in Love

Lan Chufang

(I)

His love is true,

His heart good too.

I only want him to make it clear.

If our love's known, I fear;

Gossip makes me feel shy,

Questions make me sigh.

If he's not seen, I blame he's late;

When we have met, I hesitate.

Is it true I won't satisfy him till I die?

(二)

我事事村①,

他般般丑,

丑则丑村则村意相投。

则为他丑心儿真,

博得我村情儿厚。

似这般丑眷属,

村配偶,

只除天上有。

---

① 村：蠢笨。这里是反语,意为太老实。

(II)

Stupid in all am I,

Ugly all in all is he.

Our love is true though stupid and ugly are we.

He wins my love despite his ugliness;

He loves me for my stupidity none the less.

Such a pair of ugly man and stupid wife

Cannot be found in earthly life

But in the paradise on high.

醉太平

落　魄

钟嗣成

（一）

绕前街后街，

进大院深宅。

怕有那慈悲好善小裙钗①，

请乞儿一顿饱斋②，

与乞儿绣副合欢带③，

与乞儿换副新铺盖，

将乞儿携手上阳台④。

救贫咱波奶奶！

---

① 小裙钗：小女子。
② 饱斋：饱饭。
③ 合欢带：绣着合欢花的腰带，古人认为赠人合欢，可以消除怨恨。
④ 阳台：汉代宋玉《高唐赋》写巫山神女"旦为行云，暮为行雨，朝朝暮暮，阳台之下"。阳台就成为男女欢会之地的代称。

Tune: Intoxicated in Time of Peace

A Beggar-scholar

Zhong Sicheng

(I)

I go along the street,

Enter a house and drag my feet.

I ask if there's a charitable miss

Who'd give me a hearty meal overdue,

Embroider a love-knot of bliss,

Make a coverlet new,

And go to bed hand in hand with me?

Oh! Help the poor, my dear grannie!

(二)

风流贫最好①,

村沙富难交②。

拾灰泥补砌了旧砖窑③,

开一个教乞儿市学④,

裹一顶半新不旧乌纱帽,

穿一领半长不短黄麻罩⑤,

系一条半联不断皂环绦⑥,

做一个穷风月训导⑦。

① 风流贫最好:宁愿风流而贫穷。风流:无拘无束地生活。
② 村沙富难交:不愿意和富贵而粗鲁的人结交。村沙:粗俗、愚蠢的人。
③ 砖窑:形容穷人的住处。
④ 教乞儿市学:教穷孩子读书的村学。
⑤ 黄麻罩:黄色的麻制外衣。
⑥ 皂环绦:黑色的丝腰带。
⑦ 穷风月训导:贫穷却洒脱的教书先生。风月:清风明月,形容潇洒脱俗。训导:原意指负责州县学政的官员,这里指教书先生。

(II)

The poor may be happy in love,
The rich are stupid high above.
I would repair an old brick-kiln with clay,
And open a school for beggars by day.
I'll put on a black hat half outworn,
And a yellow cloak half torn
With a disjointed belt ill at ease.
I'd teach the beggars to enjoy the moon and breeze.

哨遍

看钱奴

钱 霖

（一）

试把贤愚穷究,

看钱奴自古呼铜臭①。

徇己②苦贪求,

待不教泉货周流③。

忍包羞, 油铛④插手,

血海舒拳, 肯落他人后?

晓夜寻思机彀⑤,

缘情钩距⑥, 巧取旁搜,

蝇头⑦场上苦驱驰,

马足尘中厮追逐,

积攒下无厌就。

舍死忘生, 出乖弄丑。

① 铜臭: 有钱而品质低劣。
② 徇己: 放任自己的欲望。
③ 泉货周流: 金钱流通。
④ 油铛: 油锅。
⑤ 机彀: 机关、窍门。这里指贪求钱财的各种方法。
⑥ 钩距: 购取。
⑦ 蝇头: 比喻细小的事物, 这里特指微小的利益。

Tune: Whistling Around

The Miser

Qian Lin

(I)

Can you tell truth from lies, the foolish from the wise?

The miser stinks of gold since days of old.

He is greedy for wealth at the expense of health

As if he hated to have money circulated.

He never feels shame

To thrust his hand to snatch money out of the flame,

Or from a sea of blood upsurging high.

How could he lag behind indeed?

He contrives intrigues day and night,

And seizes money by hook

Or by crook,

And seeks profit as tiny as the head of a fly,

Or a grain of dust raised by the hoof of a steed.

Insatiable to pile up wealth to his last breath,

Careless alike of life and death,

At last he brings but shame to light.

(二)耍孩儿

安贫知足神明佑,

好聚敛多招悔尤①。

王戎遗下旧牙筹,

夜连明计算无休②。

不思日月搬乌兔③,

只与儿孙作马牛。

添消瘦,不调裯鼎④,

恣逞戈矛⑤。

---

① 悔尤:后悔,怨恨。
② 王戎遗下旧牙筹,夜连明计算无休:晋代王戎非常贪财,《晋书·王戎传》载:"(王)戎性好兴利,每自执牙筹,昼夜计算,恒若不足。"牙筹,计算用的筹码。
③ 不思日月搬乌兔:不知道时光过去得快。乌兔:指代日月。
④ 不调裯鼎:不考虑自己的衣服和饮食。裯:夹衣。鼎:古代烹饪的器皿。
⑤ 恣逞戈矛:恣意争夺钱财。

(II) Tune: Playing the Child

God helps those who, content, won't complain of poverty;

Piled-up riches invite regret and woe.

A sage with his counters of ivory

Calculated without rest night and day,

Careless if time with sun and moon will turn away.

He'd toil with all his force for his sons like a horse.

Thin he would grow,

Careless alike of his clothing and food,

Only over money would he brood.

（三）十煞

渐消磨双脸春，
已雕飕两鬓秋①。
终朝不乐眉长皱，
恨不得
柜头钱五分息招人借，
架上衵②一周年不放赎。
狠毒性如狼狗，
把平人骨肉
做自己膏油。

---

① 渐消磨双脸春，已雕飕两鬓秋：逐渐熬到老。雕飕：凋零。
② 衵：贴身衣物。从句子的意思来看，它是顾客当掉的衣物。

(III) Tune: Last Stanza But Ten

The vernal hue on his cheeks fades away;

Autumn frost is sprinkled on his hair by and by.

His gloomy eyebrows frown all the day;

He would lend at fifty per cent interest high.

He wished the goods in pawn unredeemed a year long.

As cruel as a wolf strong,

He would press oil from people's bones

In spite of their loud groans.

（四）九煞

有心待拜五侯①,

教人唤甚半州②。

忍饥寒攒得家私厚。

待垒做钱山儿

倩军士喝号提铃守③,

怕化做钱龙儿

请法官行罡布气留④。

半炊儿八遍把牙关叩⑤,

只愿得无支有管,

少出多收。

---

① 有心待拜五侯：意为想做高官。
② 半州：半个州的土地，元代大地主往往被称为半州，意为他占有半个州的土地。
③ 待垒作钱山儿倩军士喝号提铃守：把搜刮来的钱堆成山，派军士看守。倩：请。
④ 怕化作钱龙儿请法官行罡布气留：担心这些钱化作龙飞走，请道士作法留住。行罡布气：指道士作法。罡：天上极高处的风。
⑤ 半炊儿八遍把牙关叩：半顿饭工夫扣了八遍牙，形容为聚敛钱财而苦思冥想。

(IV) Tune: Last Stanza But Nine

He has a mind to be a baron high,
But he is called as "rich as half a state".
Why should he bear hunger and cold
To pile up a mountain of gold?
And hire guardsmen ringing bells at the gate
For fear his money-dragon away might fly?
He would invite Taoist priests to use magic art
To keep it from flying apart.
He snashes his teeth, walking to and fro,
Planning to have all income and no outgo.

（五）八煞

亏心事尽意为，

不义财尽力掊①，

那里问亲兄弟亲姊妹亲姑舅。

只待要春风金谷骄王恺②，

一任教夜雨新丰困马周③。

无亲旧，

只知敬明眸皓齿④，

不想共⑤肥马轻裘。

---

① 掊：聚敛。
② 只待要春风金谷骄王恺：满心期望能像石崇那样富贵骄人。《晋书·石苞传》载：石崇官荆州刺史，劫商客致富，置金谷别墅于河阳。他常与贵戚王恺争胜斗宝。武帝赐给王恺一枝二尺多高的珊瑚树，石崇随手击碎，王恺责问他，他令人拿出自己的珊瑚树，高三四尺的有六七株，王恺一时怅然自失。春风：指得意的样子。
③ "一任教"句：根本不管像马周那样贫穷困顿的人。《旧唐书·马周传》载：马周郁郁不得志，游历长安，投宿在新丰的旅店里。店主只顾供应商贩，不管马周，马周就要了一些酒，悠然独酌。
④ 明眸皓齿：指美人。
⑤ 共：借给别人。

(V) Tune: Last Stanza But Eight

He feels no shame to do what is to blame,

And injures his health for ill-gotten wealth.

He does not care for others,

Even his uncles, aunties, sisters, brothers.

He would outshine the richest man in Golden Valley fine,

But not care for the poor scholar ill at an inn.

He has no friend or kin,

He only loves the beauty with bright eyes and teeth white,

But shares with none his fur coat and carriage light.

(六)七煞

资生利转多，

贪婪意不休，

为锱铢①舍命寻争斗。

田连阡陌心犹窄，

架插诗书眼不瞅。

也学采东篱菊，

子是个装呵元亮，

豹子浮丘②。

---

① 锱铢：古代极其微小的重量单位，六铢等于一锱，四锱等于一两。
② 也学采东篱菊，子是个装呵元亮，豹子浮丘：他也学陶渊明采菊东篱，但却是作秀的，他外表善良风雅，却内心凶狠粗鄙。装呵：装模作样。元亮：陶渊明的字。豹子：元代人称凶狠的人为豹子。浮丘：传说中的仙人。

(VI) Tune: Last Stanza But Seven

"The more profit you obtain,
The more you still want to gain.
You'd carry on a strife at the risk of your life.
Though you have field on field, you are not satisfied;
On your shelf there are books on which you won't take looks.
You pretend to enjoy chrysanthemums by fenceside,
But you're a pseudo-bard,
A disguised leopard."

（七）六煞

恨不得扬子江变做酒，

枣穰金①积到斗。

为几文垫背钱②

受了些旁人咒。

一斗粟与亲眷分了颜面③，

二斤麻把相知结下寇仇。

真纰缪④，

一味的骄而且吝，

甚的是乐以忘忧！

---

① 枣穰金：枣穰般颜色的金子，赤金。
② 垫背钱：一点点小钱。垫：装裱书画的轴。
③ 分了颜面：伤了和气。
④ 纰缪：错误。

(VII) Tune: Last Stanza But Six

"You wish to turn the endless river into wine,
To pile up gold as date-palms you incline.
You're cursed by others for the money they owe you;
For a loan of millet you lose kins old and new.
For a bundle of hemp you turn friend into foe.
What woe!
You're blindly arrogant and greedy.
In the end you'll become careworn and needy."

（八）五煞

这财曾燃了董卓脐[①]，
曾枭了元载[②]头，
聚而不散遭殃咎。
怕不是堆金积玉连城富[③]，
眨眼早野草闲花满地愁。
干生受[④]，
生财有道，
受用无由。

[①] 董卓脐：董卓为王允所杀，尸体被扔在街上示众，董卓很肥大，守尸人晚上在他的肚脐中点灯，光明达旦。
[②] 元载：唐代宗时贪官，聚敛资财无数，后被杖杀。
[③] 连城富：形容十分富有，财产相当于几座城池。
[④] 干生受：白白地辛苦。干：白白地。

(VIII) Last Stanza But Five

"Fortune amassed made Han Premier burned up when dead,
And Tang Minister lose his head.
Piled-up wealth, if not distributed, would bring woe,
Though gold and jade are heaped up high from town to town,
Soon wild grass and weeds there will be overgrown.
However rich you may grow,
You will be annoyed
For the wealth unenjoyed."

（九）四煞

有一日大小运并在命宫，

死囚限缠在卯酉[①]，

甚的散得疾

子为你聚来得骤。

恰待调和新曲歌金帐，

逼临得红粉佳人坠玉楼[②]。

难收救，

一壁厢投河奔井，

一壁厢烂额焦头。

---

① 有一日大小运并在命宫，死囚限缠在卯酉：总有一天要倒霉受苦。大小运、命宫、寅卯，都是古代星相家的词汇。
② 恰待调和新曲歌金帐，逼临得红粉佳人坠玉楼：正准备演奏新曲，在金帐下歌舞取乐，却不料逼得佳人跳楼自杀。佳人，这里暗指石崇的爱妾绿珠，被孙秀逼迫坠楼自尽。

(IX) Last Stanza But Four

"One day good or ill fortune will fall by fate,
You are bound to die early or late.
Wealth will be spent faster than made.
Do not forget what's said
Of the beauty jumping down from tower of jade
Before she sang in golden tent a new song.
Do not forget what's wrong:
On the one hand women plunged into the well,
On the other men were battered pellmell."

(十)三煞

窗隔每都颩颩的飞,
椅桌每都出出的走。
金银钱米都消为尘垢。
山魈木客相呼唤,
寡宿孤辰厮趁逐①。
喧白昼,
花月妖将家人狐媚,
虚耗鬼把仓库潜偷②。

---

① 山魈木客相呼唤,寡宿孤辰厮趁逐:遭到妖魔的侵袭,厄运不断。山魈:猴的一种,面貌奇异,被看作是山林中的妖怪,木客是它的别名。寡宿孤辰:孤寡的星宿,孤单的时辰。古人认为,寡宿孤辰意味着人的孤寡。
② 花月妖将家人狐媚,虚耗鬼把仓库潜偷:花月妖魅惑了他的子弟,虚耗鬼盗窃了他的仓库。花月妖指娼妓,虚耗鬼指败家子。

(X) Last Stanza But Three

Through broken windows all away would fly,

And chairs and tables moved out in a gust,

Gold, silver, money, rice would turn to dust.

Monsters from forests and mountains would cry;

Orphan would follow Widow Star in Milky Way.

Noisy all day,

Spirits of flowers would bewitch the hosts;

Storehouses would be stolen by wasteful ghosts.

（十一）二煞

恼天公降下灾，

犯官刑系在囚。

他用钱时难参透。

待买他上木驴[①]

钉子轻轻钉，

吊脊筋钩儿浅浅钩。

便用杀难宽宥[②]，

魂飞荡荡，

魄散悠悠。

---

① 上木驴：元代的一种酷刑。
② 宽宥：得到宽恕，减轻刑罚。

(XI) Last Stanza But Two

Disasters fall from angry skies;
Guilty and put in jail, he tries
To bribe with money, but to no avail.
Nailed on the wooden ass,
In vain he begs to drive lightly the nail,
And to hang him up softly by the hook.
He can by no means be forgiven, look!
His wandering soul flies,
And then dispersed, alas!

（十二）尾

出落①他平生聚敛的情，
都写做临刑犯罪由。
将他死骨头告示
向通衢里甃②，
任他日炙风吹慢慢朽。

① 出落：拿出。
② 将他死骨头告示向通衢里甃：把他的尸骨放在大街上示众。通衢，大街。甃，砌砖、堆放。

(XII) Last Stanza

His wealth amassed all his life is put on display
To testify his guilt.
His corpse is exposed without a quilt
In public place by day,
Sunburned and wind-bitten till its decay.

蟾宫曲

山居自乐

孙周卿

草团标^①正对山凹,

山竹炊粳^②。

山水煎茶。

山芋山薯,

山葱山韭,

山果山花。

山溜响冰敲月牙^③,

扫山云^④惊散林鸦。

山色元佳,

山景堪夸。

山外晴霞,

山下人家。

---

① 草团标:圆形的茅草屋。
② 粳:刚刚收获的新谷子打出的米。
③ 山溜响冰敲月牙:山间清泉叮咚作响,犹如冰敲月牙一样。
④ 扫山云:山间云气氤氲,清风犹如在扫云。

Tune: Song of Moon Palace

Delight in the Mountain

Sun Zhouqing

In my round thatched cot in face of the valley,
I cook my rice
With bamboo of the mountain,
And brew my tea with water of the fountain.
I eat potatoes sweet, onions, chives and fruit,
And enjoy mountain flowers in view.
I listen to ice crack under the moon new;
Clouds swept away by mountain breeze
Startle crows from the trees.
The mountain hue so green,
Can I not feel proud
Of the mountain scene?
Beyond the mountains spreads the sunlit cloud;
There're cottages at the mountain's foot.

庆东原
江头即事

曹 德

低茅舍,
卖酒家,
客来旋①把朱帘挂。
长天落霞,
方池睡鸭,
老树昏鸦。
几句杜陵②诗,
一幅王维画。

① 旋:快。
② 杜陵:杜少陵的简称,即唐代大诗人杜甫。杜甫曾住在长安少陵,故后人称他为杜少陵。

Tune: Blessed Eastern Plain

The Rivershore

Cao De

Among the thatched cottages low

There is a shop selling wine.

When comes a drinker, they will soon uproll

The curtain red.

In endless sky the rainbow clouds overspread,

Ducks sleep here and there around a pond square,

Over old trees hovers crow on crow.

It's like a poetic line

Or a painter's scroll.

解三酲

真 氏

奴本是明珠擎掌①,
怎生的流落平康②?
对人前乔③做作娇模样,
背地里泪千行。
三春南国怜飘荡,
一事东风无主张。
添悲怆,
那里有珍珠十斛④,
来赎云娘⑤!

① 明珠擎掌:掌上明珠。
② 平康:唐代长安平康里,为歌伎聚居之处,后代指妓院。
③ 乔:假装。
④ 斛:古代十斗为一斛,南宋末改为五斗为一斛。
⑤ 云娘:唐传奇《裴航》载,秀才向仙女云英求婚,云英母说:"欲娶云英,须以玉杵为聘,为捣药百日乃可。"后来秀才终于实现了这个要求,娶云英而仙去。后世以云娘代指风尘女子。

Tune: Thrice Drunk and Sobered

Zhen Shi

I was a bright pearl in my parents' palm.

How could I sink low in mansions of dreams?

It is my duty to please men by my beauty,

But behind them my tears fall in streams.

Homeless for three long springs, far from the southern land,

How, driven by the east wind, could I stand?

I'm further grieved

To find no one to pay a lot of pearls as alm

That I may be relieved.

天净沙

闲 题

吴西逸

长江万里归帆,
西风几度阳关①?
依旧红尘满眼。
夕阳新雁,
此情时拍阑干②。

① 西风几度阳关:西风萧飒时节依然不停地出门做客。阳关:古代地名,王维《送元二使安西》:"西出阳关无故人。"
② 时拍阑干:牢骚满腹,抑郁愤懑的样子。辛弃疾《水龙吟·登建康赏心亭》:"把吴钩看了,栏杆拍遍,无人会,登临意。"

Tune: Sunny Sand

Written at Leisure

Wu Xiyi

On thousand-mile-long River pass east-going sails.

How many times at Sunny Pass has blown west breeze?

Still I see a world of dust to my disgust.

At sunset cry the newcome wild geese.

What can I do but beat now and then on the rails.

清江引

秋 居

吴西逸

白雁^①乱飞秋似雪,
清露生凉夜。
扫却石边云^②,
醉踏松根月,
星斗满天人睡也。

---

① 白雁:白色的雁,暗指已是深秋。
② 石边云:山中的雾气,暗指山很高。

Tune: Song of the Clear River

An Autumn Night

Wu Xiyi

White wild geese fly pell-mell like autumn snow;
In the cool night clear dew-drops grow.
Drunk, I tread on the pine-tree's root steeped in moonlight
And wipe the stone clean of cloud white.
Under the starry sky sleepy I lie.

寿阳曲

四时（秋）

吴西逸

萦①心事，
惹恨词。
更那堪动人秋思。
画楼边几声新雁儿，
不传书摆成个愁字。

① 萦：缠绕。

Tune: Song of Long-lived Sun

Four Seasons (Autumn)

Wu Xiyi

Grief heavy on my heart

Can't be written in word.

What can I do to keep autumn apart?

Beyond my painted bower is heard

The newcome wild geese's cry.

They bring no letter but write "loneliness" in the sky.

醉太平

程景初

恨绵绵深宫怨女,
情默默梦断羊车①,
冷清清长门②寂寞
长青芜。
日迟迟春风院宇,
泪漫漫介破琅玕玉③。
闷淹淹散心出户
闲凝伫,
昏惨惨晚烟妆点
雪模糊,
淅零零洒梨花暮雨。

① 羊车:史书记载晋武帝常乘坐羊车,任其在后宫行走,羊车停在哪里,他就在哪里歇宿。这里指天子的临幸。
② 长门:汉武帝皇后陈阿娇失宠后居住在长门宫,她花费重金请司马相如写了《长门赋》,又再次得宠。长门指失宠的妃子居住的冷宫。
③ 泪漫漫介破琅玕玉:深宫怨女泪水长流,能把玉石滴穿。介:断裂。琅玕:一种美玉,非常坚硬。

Tune: Drunk in Time of Peace

Cheng Jingchu

The endless grief weighs on her heart in palace deep;
In silence she dreams of royal cab drawn by sheep.
Before the lonely Gate grows green grass sad and drear;
The setting sun lingers, only spring wind comes here.
Her streams of tears have specked the jadelike bamboo;
Gloomy, she goes outdoors, having nothing to do.
She takes a stroll at leisure,
And gazes on the smoky scene without pleasure.
Oh! what she sees
Is drizzling rain and evening breeze
And petals falling from pear trees.

水仙子

无名氏

（一）

青山隐隐水茫茫，
时节登高①却异乡。
孤城孤客孤舟上，
铁石人也断肠。
泪涟涟断送了秋光。
黄花梦，
一夜香，
过了重阳。

---

① 时节登高：指农历九月九重阳节，是家人团聚登高的时候。

Tune: Song of Daffodils

Anonymous

(I)

Green hills are veiled in mist along the far-flung stream,
On Mountain-climbing Day I stand in foreign land.
A lonely man in lonely boat by lonely town,
However hard, can my heart not break down?
Two streams of tears have blurred out autumn light.
The golden dream
Is sweet but for one night.
This Mountain-climbing Day is passed just as the last.

（二）

夕阳西下水东流，
一事无成两鬓秋。
伤心人比黄花瘦①，
怯重阳②九月九。
强登临情思悠悠。
望故国三千里，
倚秋风十二楼，
没来由惹起闲愁。

---

① 人比黄花瘦：出自宋代李清照词《醉花阴》："帘卷西风，人比黄花瘦。"黄花，菊花。
② 重阳：民俗阴历九月九日是重阳节，人们登高聚会，饮酒赏花。

(II)

The sun sinks in the west while the stream eastward flows.
Nothing achieved, on my two temples white hair grows.
Heart broken, I am thinner than a yellow flower,
Fearful of the coming of Mountain-climbing Day.
Forced to climb up high, my thoughts go back to my bower
In my native land thousands of miles away.
I would lean on rails of twelve towers in autumn breeze.
Why should I be grieved and feel ill at ease?

（三）

常记的离筵饮泣饯行时，

折尽青青杨柳枝①。

欲拈斑管②书心事，

无那③可④乾坤天样般纸。

意悬悬⑤诉不尽相思，

谩⑥写下鸳鸯字，

空吟就花月词，

凭何人付与娇姿。

---

① 折尽青青杨柳枝：折柳赠行，是古代的风俗，表现离别时依依不舍的深情。
② 斑管：指用斑竹为笔管的毛笔。
③ 无那：无奈。
④ 可：整个，满。
⑤ 意悬悬：情意深切，无比挂念的样子。
⑥ 谩：徒然，白白地。

(III)

I often remember our feast of adieu
When we mingled our tears with wine new.
I would break all green willow twigs before we part,
To write down as my pen what's on my heart,
Can I find paper as big as the sky above?
Could it contain my endless regret and love?
I can only write down two words: "Love birds."
In vain I croon the love of the breeze for the moon.
On whom can I depend my love letter to send?

折桂令

无名氏

叹世间多少痴人,
多是忙人,
少是闲人。
酒色迷人,
财气昏人,
缠定①活人。
钹儿鼓儿终日送人②,
车儿马儿常时迎人③。
精细的瞒人,
本分的饶人。
不识时人,
枉只为人。

① 缠定:死死缠住。
② 钹儿鼓儿终日送人:钹儿鼓儿总是在为死去的人送行。
③ 车儿马儿常时迎人:车马总是在迎接新的重要人物到来。

Tune: Plucking Laurel Branch

Anonymous

How many in the world are people unwise?
Most of them early rise;
Few are idle guys.
Some bewitched by women and wine lose their health;
Others are greedy for wealth.
The living to death are bound;
The dead are sent to burial mound.
Carriages and horses welcome the new,
The crafty will deceive you,
The uncrafty will forgive.
If you do not know how to live,
You are a swain living in vain.

折桂令

微雪

无名氏

朔风寒吹下银沙,
蠹砌①穿帘,
拂柳惊鸦。
轻若鹅毛,
娇如柳絮,
瘦似梨花。
本应是怜贫困天教少洒,
止不过庆丰年众与农家。
数片琼葩,
点缀槎丫②。
孟浩然③容易寻梅,
陶学士不够烹茶。

---

① 蠹砌:像蠹虫一样慢慢地腐蚀了脚下的台阶。
② 槎丫:树枝。
③ 孟浩然:唐代诗人,他有雪天骑驴赏梅写诗的雅兴。

Tune: Plucking Laurel Branch

Slight Snow

Anonymous

The northern wind blows snow down like silver sand,

It erodes the steps where I stand,

Passes through the screen, caresses willow trees,

And startles crows. It's light as feather of geese,

As willow down it's tender,

And as pear flower it's slender.

Heaven pities the poor and sheds only snow slight,

To announce a bumper year to the farmers' delight.

A few jade petals in full bloom

Adorn the branches of a tree.

It would be easier for the poet to seek mume;

It's not enough for a scholar to brew his tea.

塞鸿秋

山行警

无名氏

东边路,西边路,南边路。
五里铺①,七里铺,十里铺。
行一步,盼一步,懒一步。
霎时间天也暮,
日也暮,云也暮。
斜阳满地铺,
回首生烟雾。
兀的②不山无数,
水无数,情无数。

① 铺:宋代称邮递驿站为铺,被元代沿用。
② 兀的:语气助词,反诘语,起加强语气的作用。

Tune: Autumn Swan on Frontier

On My Way in the Mountain

Anonymous

On eastern way, on western way, on southern way,

Five miles away, seven miles away, ten miles away.

I go slow-paced, I stop slow-paced, I look slow-paced.

Suddenly the sky is effaced,

The sun effaced, the clouds effaced.

The earth is paved with departing sunbeams;

Turning my head, I find mist grow as dreams.

Does mist not veil the countless hills and rills?

Does it not veil my heart which untold sorrow fills?

塞鸿秋

无名氏

爱他时似爱初生月,
喜他时似喜看梅梢月①,
想他时道几首西江月②,
盼他时似盼辰钩月。
当初意儿别,
今日相抛撇,
要相逢似水底捞明月。

---

① 梅梢月:梅与眉谐音双关,暗含"喜上眉梢"之意。
② 西江月:唐玄宗时教坊曲名,后用为词调,这里泛指填词抒情。

Tune: Autumn Swan on Frontier

Anonymous

My love for him is like moonrise,

My joy like brows above the eyes.

Thinking of him, The Moon on West River I croon;

Waiting for him, my heart is like the waning moon.

Then he was highly pleased with me.

Now forsaken by him can I be?

Our reunion is like the moon deep in the sea.

梧叶儿

嘲谎人

无名氏

东村里鸡生凤,
南庄上马变牛。
六月里裹皮裘。
瓦垄①上宜栽树,
阳沟②里好驾舟。
瓮来大肉馒头,
俺家的茄子大如斗。

① 瓦垄：房上瓦脊。
② 阳沟：屋檐下流水的明沟。

Tune: Plane Leaves

Satire on Liars

Anonymous

In eastern village phoenixes are born of cocks;
In southern farm a horse changes into an ox.
In summer we wear furs lest we should freeze;
The roof is a good place to plant trees.
In a dry moat we may sail a boat;
In a jar we may bake bread and cook meat.
My eggplant is as big as melon sweet.

梧叶儿

贪

无名氏

一夜千条计,
百年万世心①。
火院有海来深。
头枕着连城玉,
脚踩着遍地金。
有一日死来临,
问贪公哪一件儿替得您?

---

① 一夜千条计,百年万世心:描写贪婪者整夜都在谋划如何积累钱财,恨不得在短短的一生中积累起万世万代用不完的财富。

Tune: Plane Leaves

To a Greedy Man

Anonymous

You weave a thousand plots one night,
And plan for a hundred years bright.
Your pit of hell is as deep as the sea.
On precious jade you pillow your head,
On a field of gold your feet tread.
One day when death befalls you, see!
What could stand you in good stead?

四换头
相 思

无名氏

两叶眉头,
怎锁相思万种愁?
从他别后,
无心挑绣①,
这般证候②,
天知道和天瘦③。

① 挑绣:刺绣。
② 证候:模样。
③ 和天瘦:一天比一天瘦。

Tune: Changes of Tunes

(I) Lovesickness

Anonymous

With eyebrows like two willow leaves
I frown, but I can't drown my lovesickness that grieves,
Since he went away,
Absent-minded, I do embroidery all day.
If Heaven knew the state of mind I'm in,
It would also grow thin.

四换头

约 情

无名氏

东墙花月,
好景良宵恁记者。
低低的说:
来时节,
明日早些,
不志诚随灯灭①!

---

① 不志诚随灯灭:你如果对我不是真心,就会像灯灭了一样死去。旧时民间就有指灯起誓一说。

Tune: Changes of Tunes

(II) A Tryst

Anonymous

"Among flowers by the eastern wall in moonlight,
Remember such a lovely scene and lovely night!"
She whispers in his ear:
  "Come earlier tomorrow, hear!
If you love me in doubt,
You will pass away as the light goes out."

红绣鞋

无名氏

一个日请^①千钟美禄,
一个家无担石之储。
天理如何有荣枯^②?
一个三十二上居陋巷,
一个二十四考做中书,
都做了北邙山下土。

① 日请:每天进账。
② 荣枯:繁华与衰落的交替。

Tune: Embroidered Red Shoes

Anonymous

One enjoyed wealth all men adore;

Another had no food in store.

Is Heaven just or unfair?

At thirty-two one lived in a house bare;

Another became premier at twenty-four.

Now both are buried in the open air.

红绣鞋

无名氏

裁剪下才郎名讳①,
端详了展转②伤悲。
把两个字灯焰上燎成灰,
或擦在双鬓角,
或画着远山眉,
则要我眼跟前常见你。

① 名讳:名字。
② 展转:辗转。

Tune: Embroidered Red Shoes

Anonymous

Cutting down my lover's name,
I'm grieved to gaze at it again and again.
I burn to ashes these two words in candle flame,
And use them to powder my temples twain,
Or to pencil my eyebrows so that "you
Will never be out of my view."

红绣鞋

无名氏

一两句别人闲话,
三四日不把门踏。
五六日不来呵①在谁家?
七八遍买龟儿卦②,
久以后见着他,
十分的僬悴煞。

① 呵:语气词,同"啊"。
② 龟儿卦:用龟壳来占卜。

Tune: Embroidered Red Shoes

Anonymous

You have heard one gossip or two;

For three days or four you came not to my door.

For five or six you thought the gossip true.

For seven times I bought tortoise shell to divine.

When I see you after eight days or nine,

I'm languid. Do you know how much for you I pine!

红绣鞋

赠 妓

无名氏

长江水流不尽心事,

中条山隔不断情思。

想着你,

夜深沉,

人静悄,

自来时。

来时节三两句话,

去时节一篇词,

记在你心窝儿里直到死①。

---

① 本曲后半段与贯云石的《红绣鞋》类似。

Tune: Embroidered Red Shoes

For a Songstress

Anonymous

The Long River can't carry my longing away;

The Middle Mountain can't bar our love in midway.

Deep, deep I think of you

In deep night of adieu.

Silence reigns far and nigh.

When you came by,

You said two words or three,

When you left me,

You left but a verse free.

I'll bear it in mind till I die.

庆宣和

无名氏

寄语寒窗老秀才,
一经①头白,
更等甚三年选场②开?
去来,
去来!

① 一经:"五经"中《诗》《书》《礼》《易》《春秋》之一,指专注于"五经"中的一本。
② 选场:科举考试。

Tune: Celebration of Imperial Reign

Anonymous

I tell the old unsuccessful candidate:
   "Do not study too late!
One classic read, white hair grows on your head.
Why should you wait for three years for another exam?
Learn from what I am!
Do not participate!

沉醉东风

无名氏

（一）

安排下歌喉舞腰,
准备着月夕花朝。
恨春过,
伤春早,
且休交①燕莺知道,
春色三分二分了②。
莫惜花间醉倒。

---

① 交：让。
② 春色三分二分了：春色三分，已经过去了二分，指春天很快就要过去了。

Tune: Intoxicated in East Wind

Anonymous

(I)

Songstress' throat tender

And dancer's waist slender

Are ready for flowers in the light of the moon.

I regret spring has passed too soon.

Let it not to swallows and orioles be known

That two-thirds of spring have gone away.

It's better to be drunk before flowers by day.

（二）

俺三竿日身披衲甲^①,
恁五更寒帽裹乌纱。
俺耕耘阔角牛,
恁嘶月高头马。
俺打勤劳不羡荣华,
恁苦战垓心血染沙。
俺老瓦盆边醉煞。

① 衲甲：破旧的盔甲。

(II)

I'd wear my patched coat when the sun is high;
Your official hat is not cold-proof at midnight.
I'd till my field with my buffalo under the sky,
You might ride your steed neighing in moonlight.
I would toil hard and envy none who shine;
You might on blood-stained ground put up a fight.
I would lie drunk by the side of my jar of wine.

塞儿令

无名氏

有钱时唤小哥,

无钱也失人情。

好家私伴着些歹后生,

卖弄他聪明。

一关的胡行①。

踢气球养鹌鹑,

解库②中不想营生。

包服内响钞精钞③。

但行处,

十数个花街里做郎君

则由他胡子传柳隆卿④。

---

① 一关的胡行:一味胡作非为。
② 解库:当铺。
③ 响钞精钞:指成色好的银子。
④ 胡子传、柳隆卿:元代杂剧、南戏中经常出现的无赖恶少或帮闲人物。

Tune: Song of Frontier

Anonymous

Rich, you are called dear brothers;
Penniless, you're despised by others.
Good fortune's left to worthless son
Showing off clever things he's done.
It has proved of little avail
To kick the shuttlecock or play with quail.
He would not earn a living in his pawn shop,
But spend his money hard and soft without stop.
He has visited brothels from door to door
Till destitute, he is driven out by the whore.

上小楼

杜鹃

无名氏

堪恨无情杜宇,
你怎么伤人心绪?
啼的花残,
叫的愁来,
唤将春去。
索甚①不把离人叮咛嘱咐,
我也道在天涯不如归去。

① 索甚:为什么。

Tune: Ascending the Attic

The Cuckoo

Anonymous

I do not like to hear pitiless cuckoo cry,

Its home-going song breaks my heart.

It cries till no flowers bloom,

Till grief comes with gloom,

Till spring from earth will part.

"Why don't you tell my love at the end of the sky,

To come home lest I should die?"

寄生草

无名氏

有几句知心话,
本待要诉与他。
对神前剪下青丝发,
背爹娘暗约在湖山下。
冷清清,
湿透凌波袜①,
恰相逢和我意儿差②。
不剌③你不来时
还我香罗帕。

① 凌波袜:袜子。曹植《洛神赋》:"凌波微步,罗袜生尘。"
② 恰相逢和我意儿差:才见面就发现,他的心情和我很不同。恰:才。差:不一样。
③ 不剌:感叹词,罢了、算了。

Tune: Parasite Grass

Palace Grief

Anonymous

I would impart

To you what's in my heart.

Before God I cut down a wreath of my hair black.

Behind my parents we tryst at the foot of the hill,

Lonely and still,

With dew my stockings are wet.

Hardly have we met when we disagree.

If you regret,

Give back

My fragrant handkerchief to me!

快活三过朝天子四换头

无名氏

（一）快活三

良辰美景换今古，
赏心乐事暗乘除。
人生四事①岂能无？
不可教轻辜负。

---

① 人生四事：指生、老、病、死。

From "Happy Three" to "Changes of Tunes"

Anonymous

(I) Tune: Happy Three

Oh, lovely times and charming scenes change by and by;
Alas! the delights to the heart will pass away.
Man is fated to live, grow old, fall ill and die.
So let us make the most of each hour and each day!

（二）朝天子

唤取伴侣

正好向西湖路。

花前沉醉倒玉壶，

香喷雾，红飞雨。

九十韶华，人间客寓①。

把三分分数数：

一分是流水，

二分是尘土，

不觉的春将暮②。

---

① 人间客寓：形容人生就像在世上做客。
② 把三分分数数：一分是流水，二分是尘土，不觉的春将暮：化用宋代苏轼《水龙吟》词句："春色三分，二分尘土，一分流水。"

(II) Tune: Skyward Song

O call a friend

And go on our way to West Lake today!

Let us drink up the pot of jade to the end!

Fragrant mist spread,

Petals fall red.

Even if you can live to ninety years,

The world still like an inn appears.

Count the three spring graces like dreams:

One-third passes with flowing streams;

Two-thirds with the dust.

Without our knowledge spring will pass in a gust.

（三）四换头

西园杖履，
望眼无穷恨有余。
飘残香絮，
歌残白苎①。
海棠花底鹧鸪，
杨柳梢头杜宇，
都唤取春归去。

① 白苎：苎麻，多年生草本植物。

(III) Tune: Change of Tunes

In the west garden, cane in hand,

With endless grief I gaze into the far-off land.

Dancers are gone with fragrant willow down;

Songstress tired in her white silk gown.

Under crabapple flowers partridges cry;

Over willow tops cuckoos fly.

All call spring back and say "Goodbye!"

阅金经

无名氏

一竿①为活计,
往来西又东。
笑着荷衣不叹穷。
翁,
醉眠杨柳风。
波微动,
晚来舟自横②。

① 竿:钓鱼竿。
② 晚来舟自横:化用唐朝韦应物诗《滁州西涧》:"春潮带雨晚来急,野渡无人舟自横。"

Tune: Reading Golden Classics

Anonymous

With fishing rod I earn a living without rest,
Coming and going east and west.
Wearing a straw cloak, I don't sigh
For I am poor. Old and drunk, I
Lie down in the breeze under willow trees.
On rippling waves afloat,
At dusk athwart the stream lies my boat.

普天乐

无名氏

他生的脸儿峥①,
庞儿正。
诸余里耍俏②,
所事里聪明。
忒可憎③,
没薄幸。
行里坐里茶里饭里和随定④,
恰便似纸幡儿引了人魂灵。
想那些个滋滋味味,
风风韵韵,
老老成成。

① 峥:端正,姣好。
② 诸余里耍俏:哪里都长得标志。诸余里:所事里、到处、所有的地方都。
③ 可憎:反语,指可爱。
④ 和随定:紧紧地跟随着。

Tune: Universal Joy

Anonymous

He is born with a fair, fine face,

Handsome in all, clever in word.

Lovely when he is heard,

Fickle in all he says.

Wherever he goes or stays,

Drinks or eats, I like his manner,

And follow him as a shadow under a banner.

I consider it as a favor

To absorb his flavor.

When he is honest, I appreciate his grace.

雁儿落过得胜令

愁 怀

无名氏

（一）雁儿落

一年老一年①,
一日没一日。
一秋又一秋,
一辈催一辈。

（二）得胜令②

一聚一离别,
一喜一伤悲。
一榻一身卧,
一生一梦里。
寻一伙相识,
他一会，咱一会；
都一般相知,
吹一会,
唱一会。

① 一年老一年：人一年比一年老。
② 得胜令：这是一首嵌字曲，游戏笔墨中透露出游戏人生的旷达与无奈。

From "Falling Swan" to "Triumphant Song"

Anonymous

(I) Tune: Falling Swan

From year to year we have grown old,
And day after day time is sold.
One autumn comes when another goes;
One generation after another grows.

(II) Tune: Triumphant Song

We meet and part
With joy or broken heart.
With a bed to lie on,
Our life is but a dream bygone.
Find a group of companions:
Now he or she,
Now you and me.
For friends we all shall be.
Now let's blow short or long,
Now let us sing a song.

叨叨令

无名氏

黄尘万古长安路①,
折碑②三尺邙山③墓。
西风一叶乌江④渡,
夕阳十里邯郸树⑤。
老了人也么哥,
老了人也么哥,
英雄尽是伤心处。

---

① 黄尘万古长安路:千百年来,多少人为求取功名而奔走于去往长安的路上。黄尘:形容人马喧闹,道路上尘土飞扬。万古:夸张手法,指时间久远。
② 折碑:断掉的墓碑。
③ 邙山:在河南洛阳市东北,汉朝以来,许多王公贵族埋葬于此,泛指墓地。
④ 乌江:西楚霸王项羽兵败自刎的地方。
⑤ 邯郸树:唐代沈既济的《枕中记》写道,卢生做了一个美梦,醒来时却只见夕阳和古树。

Tune: Chattering Song

Anonymous

Yellow dust raised on royal road since olden days,

The graveside ruins steeped in departing sunrays.

A leaf falls on Black River with the western breeze,

The setting sun sheds light for miles on dreaming trees.

How can we not grow old?

How can we not grow old?

All hearts are broken for the heroes bold.

叨叨令

无名氏

溪边小径舟横渡①,
门前流水清如玉。
青山隔断红尘路②,
白云满地无寻处。
说与你寻不得也么哥③,
寻不得也么哥。
却原来侬家鹦鹉洲边住。

① 渡:渡口,摆渡处。
② 红尘路:通往喧嚣俗世的道路。
③ 也么哥:语尾助词,有加强语气的作用。

Tune: Chattering Song

Anonymous

I cross the stream and follow the creekside pathway,
And reach the door where runs water jade-clear.
The green hills screen it from the world of dust red;
It can't be found for the ground's with clouds overspread.
I tell you it can't be found, my dear;
It can't be found, my dear.
In my cottage on Parrot Isle with none I'd stay.

游四门

无名氏

（一）

落红满地湿胭脂^①,
游赏正宜时。
呆才料^②不顾蔷薇刺,
贪折海棠枝。
支!
抓破绣裙儿。

---

① 胭脂：形容春雨过后，满地的落花像胭脂一样。
② 呆才料：呆子，对爱人的昵称。才料，即材料。

Tune: The Four Gates Visited

Anonymous

(I)

The fallen reds on the ground look like a rouged face.

It's the best time to visit vernal place.

You fool don't know the rose has thorn,

But try to pluck crabapple flowers down.

See! My silk gown

Is suddenly torn.

（二）

海棠花下月明时，
有约暗通私。
不付能①等得红娘至。
欲审旧题诗。
支！
关上角门儿。

---

① 不付能：元曲中常用的词，意为没料到。

(II)

In moonlight steeped crabapple flowers,
I have a tryst between the secret bowers.
Impatiently I wait for the one I adore,
Reading again the billet when comes Rose
To close
The corner door.

三番玉楼人

无名氏

风摆檐间马,
雨打响碧窗纱,
枕剩衾寒没乱煞①。
不着我题名儿骂②。
暗想他,
忒情杂,
等来家,
好生的歹斗咱。
我将那厮脸儿上不抓,
耳轮儿揪罢,
我问你昨夜宿谁家?

① 没乱煞:急死人。
② 不着我题名儿骂:我怎么能不指着名字骂呢!从这句开始,这是描述主人公等待得不耐烦的一系列心理活动。

Tune: Thrice in Jade Pavilion

Anonymous

Bells hanging on the eaves ring in the breeze;

Rain beats loud on the green window without cease.

How can I bear alone the quilt and pillow cold!

How can I not blame the ungrateful gallant bold!

I can't keep him apart

With his divided heart.

Should he come to my place,

I would scold him without giving him grace,

Scratch him on the face.

And pinch his ears tight.

I'd ask him, "With whom did you pass the night?"

朝天子

志 感

无名氏

不读书有权,

不识字有钱,

不晓事倒有人夸荐。

老天只恁忒心偏,

贤和愚无分辨。

折挫英雄,

消磨良善,

越聪明越运蹇①。

志高如鲁连②,

德过如闵骞③,

依本分只落的人轻贱。

---

① 运蹇:运气不好。蹇:跛脚。
② 鲁连:鲁仲连,战国时齐国人,善于谋略,曾为赵国破解了秦国的围困,但不愿意出仕,被认为是志行高洁。
③ 闵骞:闵子骞,孔子的弟子,以德行著称。

Tune: Skyward Song

Reflections

Anonymous

Those who can't read are powerful,
Those who can't write pass wealthy days,
The ignorant may win high praise.
Is it not Heaven's care to be just and fair?
How can he not know the good from the fool?
Why are heroes often frustrated
And talents not utilized?
The better they're, the worse they're fated.
What is the use to solve dispute
Or have a virtue mute?
If you but do your duty, you will be despised.

叨叨令

无名氏

不思量尤在心头记,
越思量越恁地添憔悴。
香罗帕揾不住腮边泪。
几时节笑吟吟
成了鸳鸯配。
兀的不盼杀人也么哥!
兀的不盼杀人也么哥!
咱两个武陵溪畔
曾相识。

Tune: Chattering Song

Anonymous

Though I don't think of you, you appear in my heart;

When I think of you, can I keep languor apart?

How can my fragrant silk handkerchief stay

My tears streaming down from my eyes?

When can we beam with smiles and realize

Our love-birds' dream?

How can I not wish for such a happy day?

How can I not wish for such a happy day!

We who were happy by the side of lovely stream.

红绣鞋

无名氏

窗外雨声声不住,
枕边泪点点长吁。
雨声泪点急相逐①,
雨声儿添凄惨,
泪点儿助长吁。
枕边泪倒多如窗外雨。

---

① 逐:指不互相让,这里运用了夸张的手法。

Tune: Embroidered Red Shoes

Anonymous

Outside the window rain drips drop on drop;

Upon the pillow tears mingle with sigh on sigh.

Rain and tears hasten to fall without stop.

Rain makes the day more drear;

Tears with sighs seem to vie.

The window's not so wet as pillow with tear on tear.

喜春来

闺 情

无名氏

窄裁衫裉安排瘦,
淡扫蛾眉准备愁。
思君一度一登楼。
凝望久,
雁过楚天秋。

Tune: Welcome to Spring

Longing

Anonymous

I cut tight coat and skirt for fear I should grow thin;
I lightly pencil my brows to hide my chagrin.
O When I long for you, I mount the tower high,
Stand long and gaze far and nigh,
But I see only wild geese crossing autumn sky.

快活三过朝天子四换头

忆 别

无名氏

（一）快活三

人去后敛翠颦①，
春归也掩朱门。
日长庭静怕黄昏，
又是愁时分。

① 敛翠颦：指少妇愁眉不展的样子。

From "Happy Three" to "Changes of Tunes"

Parting Grief

Anonymous

(I) Tune: Happy Three

Since he left me, my brows are often knit.
When spring is gone, I close my red door.
The day is long in courtyard still, how can I bear it
For dusk is the time to deplore.

（二）朝天子

新痕，

旧痕，

泪滴尽愁难尽。

今宵鸳帐睡怎稳？

口儿念心儿印，

独上妆楼，

无人存问①。

见花梢月半轮，

望频，

断魂。

正人远天涯近。

① 存问：安慰。

(II) Tune: Skyward Song

New traces and old
Of countless tears and grief untold,
How can I in lovebirds bed fall asleep?
You're printed on my lips and in my heart deep.
Alone I mount the tower high,
None cares for me.
I see the new moon atop the blooming tree.
With broken heart I gaze afar,
But I can't find where you are.
Oh, are you farther away than the sky?

（三）四换头

长空成阵，
雁字行行点暮云。
早是①多离多恨，
多愁多闷。
叮咛的嘱君：
若见俺那人，
早寄取个平安信。

① 早是：本该是，原来是。

(III) Tune: Changes of Tunes

The endless sky is

Barred with evening clouds and rows of wild geese.

We part more often than we meet;

My grief is longer than joy sweet.

I tell wild geese again and again, "If you see

My man, will you please

Tell him to write a word to me?"

骂玉郎过感皇恩采茶歌

无名氏

（一）骂玉郎

四时唯有春无价，
尊日月富年华。
垂杨影里人如画。
锦一攒①，
绣一堆，
在秋千下。

---

① 一攒：一簇，一堆。

From "Blaming My Gallant" to "Tea-picking Song"

Anonymous

(I) Tune: Blaming My Gallant

Of the four seasons only spring
Is dear and priceless;
The days are bright when sun and moon shine.
Maidens under willows look like a picture fine;
Some in brocade and others in silk dress,
All gather around the swing.

（二）感皇恩

语笑欣恰[①]，

炒闹喧哗。

软红乡，

簇定[②]个，

小宫娃。

彩绳款拈，

画板轻蹅，

微着力，

身慢举，

拽裙纱。

---

① 欣恰：欢欣融洽。
② 簇定：簇拥。

(II) Tune: Gratitude to the Emperor

They talk in cheerful voice,

And make a lively noise.

Among them there's a palace maiden fair

Wearing a silk dress soft and red.

She grasps with grace the rope of colored thread,

And slightly pushes forward the swing,

Which goes as on the wing.

Her body slowly rises in the air.

Behold!

Her apron gauze still in her hold.

（三）采茶歌

众矜夸^①,
是交加^②。
彩云飞上日边霞。
体态轻盈那^③闲雅,
精神羞落树头花。

① 矜夸：骄傲。
② 交加：喧闹，纷乱。
③ 那：更加上。

(III) Tea-picking Song

All maidens vie

In swinging high.

Like rainbow clouds near to the sun they fly,

With body light and spirit bright,

Their grace would make the blooming trees feel shy.

图书在版编目（CIP）数据

许渊冲译元曲三百首：汉文、英文 /（元）关汉卿著；许渊冲译. -- 北京：中译出版社，2021.4（2022.7重印）
（许渊冲英译作品）
ISBN 978-7-5001-6442-5

Ⅰ. ①许… Ⅱ. ①关… ②许… Ⅲ. ①元曲－选集－汉、英 Ⅳ. ①I222.9

中国版本图书馆CIP数据核字(2020)第242947号

出版发行	中译出版社
地　　址	北京市西城区新街口外大街28号普天德胜大厦主楼4层
电　　话	(010)68359719
邮　　编	100088
电子邮箱	book@ctph.com.cn
网　　址	http://www.ctph.com.cn
出版人	乔卫兵
总策划	刘永淳
责任编辑	刘香玲　张　旭
文字编辑	王秋璎　张莞嘉　赵浠彤
营销编辑	毕竞方
中文注释	周晓宇
封面制作	刘　哲
内文制作	黄　浩　冯　兴
印　　刷	北京顶佳世纪印刷有限公司
经　　销	新华书店
规　　格	840mm×1092mm　1/32
印　　张	19.25
字　　数	420千
版　　次	2021年4月第1版
印　　次	2022年7月第4次

ISBN 978-7-5001-6442-5　定价：**76.00元**

版权所有　侵权必究
中译出版社